I0440303

INTRODUCTION TO
ARTIFICIAL INTELLIGENCE
UNDERSTANDING THE BASICS

A COMPREHENSIVE GUIDE TO ARTIFICIAL INTELLIGENCE

KONSTANTIN TITOV

Published by First BCI University
8345 NW 66 Street, Suite A5713
Miami, FL-33166
U.S.A.

Tel.: +1 (305) 515-6080
E-mail: firstbci@yahoo.com

Contents

Introduction to AI

Definition and History of Artificial Intelligence

Artificial Intelligence, often abbreviated as AI, is a field of computer science that has captured the imagination of technologists, researchers, and the general public alike. AI has witnessed remarkable growth and development over the past few decades, and its impact on various aspects of our lives is becoming increasingly evident. In this comprehensive exploration of AI, we will delve into its definition, historical roots, key milestones, and the ongoing evolution of this field.

Definition of Artificial Intelligence

Artificial Intelligence, as the name suggests, refers to the creation of intelligent agents or systems that can perform tasks typically requiring human intelligence. These tasks include learning, reasoning, problem-solving, understanding natural language, and perception. AI systems are designed to mimic or replicate human cognitive functions, enabling them to analyze data, make decisions, and adapt to changing circumstances.

One of the key goals of AI is to develop machines capable of autonomous learning and problem-solving without explicit programming. This ability to learn from data and improve over time is central to the field of AI and distinguishes it from traditional computer programming. AI systems can be classified into various subfields, including machine learning, natural language processing, computer vision, robotics, and expert systems, among others.

History of Artificial Intelligence

The history of AI dates to ancient times when humans began to dream of creating mechanical beings that could mimic human behavior. However, the formal study of AI as a scientific discipline began in the mid-20th century, marked by significant milestones and breakthroughs.

The Dartmouth Workshop (1956)

- The birth of AI as a field is often credited to the Dartmouth Workshop in 1956. It was organized by John McCarthy, Marvin Minsky, Nathaniel Rochester, and Claude Shannon. The workshop aimed to explore the potential of creating intelligent machines and formalized the concept of AI.

Early AI Programs (1950s-1960s)

- In the late 1950s and 1960s, AI pioneers developed early AI programs that demonstrated simple problem-solving and language understanding capabilities. Programs like the Logic Theorist and General Problem Solver laid the foundation for future AI research.

The AI Winter (1970s-1980s)

- Despite initial enthusiasm, progress in AI research faced challenges during the 1970s and 1980s, leading to what is now known as the "AI winter." Funding and interest in AI dwindled due to unrealistic expectations and limited computational power.

Expert Systems (1980s)

- During the AI winter, expert systems emerged as a prominent AI subfield. These systems utilized knowledge engineering to mimic human expertise in specific domains, such as medical diagnosis and financial analysis.

Machine Learning Renaissance (1990s)

- The 1990s saw a resurgence of interest in AI, driven by advances in machine learning techniques. Neural networks, support vector machines, and probabilistic models paved the way for more robust AI applications.

Deep Learning and Big Data (2010s)

- The 2010s witnessed a revolution in AI with the advent of deep learning, a subfield of machine learning that utilizes artificial neural networks with many layers. Deep learning, combined with the availability of large datasets, led to breakthroughs in computer vision, natural language processing, and speech recognition.

AI in Everyday Life (Present)

- Today, AI is an integral part of our daily lives. AI-powered virtual assistants like Siri and Alexa, recommendation systems, autonomous vehicles, and healthcare applications are just a few examples of AI applications that have become ubiquitous.

The Evolution of AI

Over the years, AI has undergone a significant evolution, transitioning from rule-based expert systems to complex machine learning and deep learning models. This remarkable transformation has been propelled by remarkable advances in computer hardware, the accessibility of vast datasets, and pioneering algorithmic developments. These key elements have played a pivotal role in driving the ongoing evolution of AI technology.

Machine Learning: Machine learning, a subset of AI, has been a game-changer in various industries. It encompasses supervised, unsupervised, and reinforcement learning, enabling machines to make predictions, classify data, and optimize decision-making processes.

Deep Learning: Deep learning, powered by neural networks with multiple layers, has revolutionized computer vision, natural language understanding, and speech recognition. Convolutional Neural Networks (CNNs) and Recurrent Neural Networks (RNNs) have proven instrumental in these areas.

Natural Language Processing (NLP): NLP has made significant strides in enabling machines to understand and generate human language. Chatbots, language translation services, and sentiment analysis tools are examples of NLP applications.

Computer Vision: AI has made remarkable progress in computer vision, allowing machines to interpret and process visual data. This has led to advancements in facial recognition, object detection, and autonomous navigation in robotics.

Reinforcement Learning: Reinforcement learning has enabled AI systems to learn through trial and error, making it suitable for tasks like game playing, robotics, and autonomous decision-making.

AI in Healthcare: AI has been leveraged in the healthcare sector for disease diagnosis, drug discovery, and personalized treatment plans. Machine learning models can analyze medical images, such as X-rays and MRIs, with high accuracy.

Autonomous Vehicles: Self-driving cars and autonomous drones are examples of AI-powered technologies that have the potential to revolutionize transportation and logistics.

Ethical and Social Considerations: The ethical implications of AI, including bias in algorithms and concerns about job displacement, have become central topics of discussion. Researchers and engineers are actively working to address these challenges.

The Future of AI

As an AI engineer with two decades of experience, I am excited about the future of AI. The field is poised for continued growth and innovation, with several key trends and developments on the horizon.

AI and Healthcare: AI will continue to play a crucial role in healthcare, aiding in early disease detection, drug development, and personalized treatment plans. Telemedicine and AI-powered diagnostics will become more prevalent.

AI in Education: AI-driven educational tools will provide personalized learning experiences for students. Intelligent tutoring systems and adaptive learning platforms will cater to individual learning needs.

AI and Climate Change: AI can contribute to environmental sustainability by optimizing energy consumption, predicting climate patterns, and supporting the development of green technologies.

AI in Cybersecurity: AI will be essential in identifying and mitigating cybersecurity threats. Machine learning algorithms can detect unusual patterns and vulnerabilities in real-time.

Human-AI Collaboration: The future of work will involve increased collaboration between humans and AI systems. AI will assist in complex decision-making and data analysis, enhancing productivity across industries.

AI Ethics and Regulation: Stricter regulations and ethical guidelines will be established to ensure responsible AI development and deployment. Bias mitigation and transparency will be central concerns.

Quantum Computing and AI: The emergence of quantum computing will have a profound impact on AI, enabling faster and more complex calculations. Quantum AI algorithms are being developed to leverage this technology.

Artificial Intelligence is a dynamic field that has evolved significantly since its inception in the 1950s. From early AI programs and expert systems to recent advancements in deep learning and machine learning, AI has transformed technology interaction and holds the potential to reshape various industries. The possibilities and challenges in the world of AI continue to inspire professionals. As AI continues to integrate into our lives, it offers both opportunities and hurdles that will shape the future landscape of technology and automation.

Types of AI: Narrow AI, General AI, and Superintelligent AI

Artificial Intelligence (AI) is a rapidly evolving field with diverse technologies and applications. Three primary AI categories exist, each reflecting distinct levels of intelligence and capability: Narrow AI, General AI, and Superintelligent AI.

Narrow AI specializes in specific tasks, General AI possesses human-like abilities across various domains, and Superintelligent AI surpasses human intelligence. Understanding these AI categories is fundamental in comprehending the scope and potential of AI technologies in our rapidly changing world.

Narrow AI (Weak AI)

Narrow AI, often referred to as Weak AI, represents the most common and prevalent form of artificial intelligence in use today. This type of AI is designed to perform specific tasks and solve particular problems. It operates within well-defined boundaries and lacks the broader cognitive abilities of human intelligence.

Characteristics of Narrow AI

Specialized Functions: Narrow AI is engineered for a specific purpose or domain. It excels in tasks such as image recognition, speech recognition, language translation, and recommendation systems.

Limited Context: It can only operate within the context for which it was developed. For example, a chatbot designed for customer service may struggle with understanding unrelated topics.

Lack of Self-awareness: Narrow AI lacks consciousness, self-awareness, and general understanding. It operates solely based on predefined algorithms and data.

Examples: Virtual assistants like Siri and Alexa, spam filters, and autonomous vehicles are examples of Narrow AI applications.

11

General AI (Strong AI)

General AI, also known as Strong AI or AGI (Artificial General Intelligence), represents a level of artificial intelligence that possesses human-like cognitive abilities. Unlike Narrow AI, which is specialized in one domain, General AI has the potential to understand, learn, and apply knowledge across a wide range of tasks and domains.

Characteristics of General AI

Cognitive Flexibility: General AI can adapt to various tasks and domains, demonstrating problem-solving skills, learning capabilities, and reasoning abilities similar to humans.

Self-awareness: It possesses a level of self-awareness and consciousness, allowing it to understand its own existence and make autonomous decisions.

Creative Thinking: General AI can engage in creative thinking, innovation, and abstract reasoning, going beyond predefined algorithms and data.

Ethical Considerations: The development of General AI raises ethical questions and challenges related to the potential for self-aware machines and their moral decision-making capabilities.

Ongoing Research: Achieving true General AI remains a significant challenge in the field, and researchers continue to explore avenues for its development.

Superintelligent AI

Superintelligent AI represents a theoretical concept that extends beyond General AI. It envisions AI systems with intelligence surpassing not only human capabilities but also the combined intelligence of all humanity. This level of AI remains speculative and is the subject of much debate and speculation within the AI community.

Characteristics of Superintelligent AI

Unprecedented Intelligence: Superintelligent AI would possess levels of intelligence, problem-solving, and decision-making that exceed human capacities in every conceivable way.

Advanced Learning: It would have the ability to rapidly acquire knowledge, understand complex concepts, and innovate at a pace far beyond human capabilities.

Ethical and Existential Concerns: Achieving Superintelligent AI raises profound ethical and existential concerns. Ensuring that such AI systems align with human values and interests is a paramount challenge.

Theoretical Development: The concept of Superintelligent AI is currently in the realm of science fiction and theoretical speculation. Achieving this level of AI, if possible, is considered a distant and uncertain future goal.

The AI Engineer's Perspective

Let's now explore the practical applications and challenges that are associated with these different types of artificial intelligence within the field.

Narrow AI in Everyday Life: Narrow AI systems are prevalent in our daily lives, from virtual assistants that understand voice commands to recommendation algorithms that suggest products and content. These AI applications enhance user experiences and provide valuable services.

Challenges in Achieving General AI: Developing General AI remains one of the most complex and ambitious goals in the field of AI. It requires creating systems that can not only perform tasks but also understand context, reason, and adapt to new situations.

Ethical Considerations: As AI technologies advance, ethical considerations become increasingly important. Ensuring that AI systems respect privacy, avoid bias, and make ethical decisions is an ongoing challenge.

Theoretical Exploration of Superintelligent AI: Superintelligent AI remains a topic of theoretical exploration and debate. It prompts discussions about the potential implications of highly advanced AI systems on society and humanity as a whole.

The field of Artificial Intelligence encompasses three primary types: Narrow AI, General AI, and the theoretical concept of Superintelligent AI. **Narrow AI** is currently the most prevalent form, focusing on specific tasks and domains. **General AI** represents a higher level of AI that possesses human-like cognitive abilities and adaptability. **Superintelligent AI**, while a fascinating concept, remains speculative and raises significant ethical and existential questions.

As AI continues to advance, it is essential to consider the implications of these different AI types on society, ethics, and the future of technology. AI engineers, researchers, and policymakers must work collaboratively to navigate the challenges and opportunities presented by these evolving forms of intelligence in the world of artificial intelligence.

What is Data?

Types of Data: Structured, Unstructured, Semi-Structured

Data is the lifeblood of the digital age, driving decision-making, innovation, and technological advancements across various industries.

Understanding the concept of data and its different types is fundamental not only for English language comprehension but also for comprehending the foundations of modern computing and artificial intelligence.

In this chapter, we will delve into the definition of data and examine the three primary types of data: Structured, Unstructured, and Semi-Structured.

What is Data?

Data refers to raw facts, information, or observations that are collected, recorded, or represented in a form suitable for processing and analysis. Data can take various forms, such as numbers, text, images, and more, and it serves as the foundation for generating knowledge and insights. In essence, data is the fuel that powers the engines of modern computing and artificial intelligence.

Types of Data

1. Structured Data

Structured data is organized and highly formatted, making it easy to store, retrieve, and analyze. This type of data conforms to a predefined schema or data model, which specifies the data's format, relationships, and constraints. Structured data is typically found in relational databases, spreadsheets, and other tabular formats.

Characteristics of Structured Data

Tabular Format: Structured data is often represented in tables, with rows and columns, making it suitable for databases and spreadsheet applications.

Well-Defined Schema: It adheres to a strict schema, which defines the data types, relationships between data elements, and constraints.

Examples: Customer information in a database, financial records, and inventory lists are common examples of structured data.

Easy to Query: Structured data is easily queried using SQL (Structured Query Language) or similar database query languages, allowing for efficient data retrieval and analysis.

2. Unstructured Data

Unstructured data, on the other hand, lacks a predefined structure or format. It encompasses a wide range of data types, including text documents, images, audio files, videos, and more. Unstructured data is characterized by its complexity and variability, making it challenging to analyze using traditional database methods.

Characteristics of Unstructured Data

Lack of Structure: Unstructured data does not follow a specific schema or format, making it inherently flexible and diverse.

Natural Language: Text documents, such as emails, social media posts, and articles, are common examples of unstructured data. These documents are written in natural language and may contain a mix of structured and unstructured elements.

Complexity: Analyzing unstructured data often requires advanced techniques, such as natural language processing (NLP) and computer vision, to extract meaningful insights.

Examples: Social media posts, customer reviews, image files, and audio recordings are all forms of unstructured data.

AI and Unstructured Data: AI technologies, including machine learning and deep learning, excel at extracting valuable information from unstructured data sources, enabling sentiment analysis, image recognition, and more.

3. Semi-Structured Data

Semi-structured data represents a middle ground between structured and un-

structured data. It exhibits some level of structure, often in the form of tags, labels, or hierarchical relationships, while still allowing for variability and flexibility. Semi-structured data is commonly encountered in various domains, including web content, XML documents, JSON files, and NoSQL databases.

Characteristics of Semi-Structured Data

Flexible Structure: Semi-structured data may include elements with varying structures, but it maintains a level of organization through tags or metadata.

Hierarchy: Data elements within semi-structured data may be organized hierarchically, allowing for the representation of complex relationships.

Examples: XML (eXtensible Markup Language) and JSON (JavaScript Object Notation) are well-known examples of semi-structured data formats. They are widely used for data exchange in web applications and APIs.

No Fixed Schema: Unlike structured data, semi-structured data does not adhere to a rigid schema. New elements can be added without altering the entire structure.

AI and Semi-Structured Data: AI systems can parse and extract information from semi-structured data sources, facilitating data integration and interoperability in diverse applications.

The AI Engineer's Perspective

The critical role of data in training and deploying AI models is paramount. Various data types have specific implications for AI projects, shaping their outcomes and effectiveness.

Structured Data in AI: Structured data is often used as the foundation for training machine learning models. The well-defined schema and tabular format make it suitable for tasks like predictive analytics, classification, and regression.

Unstructured Data in AI: Unstructured data presents both opportunities and challenges for AI. Natural language processing (NLP) and computer vision techniques enable AI systems to analyze and extract valuable insights from

text, images, and other unstructured sources.

Semi-Structured Data in AI: Semi-structured data is common in data integration and web-based applications. AI systems can utilize this data to provide flexible and adaptive services, such as personalized recommendations and content retrieval.

Data is the foundation of modern computing and artificial intelligence. Understanding the different types of data—Structured, Unstructured, and Semi-Structured—is essential for effectively harnessing the power of data-driven technologies. Structured data is highly organized and suitable for traditional database applications. Unstructured data encompasses a wide range of formats and requires advanced AI techniques for analysis. Semi-structured data strikes a balance between structure and flexibility, making it versatile for various applications.

As technology continues to evolve, data remains at the forefront of innovation, and AI engineers and data scientists play a pivotal role in extracting meaningful insights from the diverse data landscape. Whether structured, unstructured, or semi-structured, data is a valuable resource that drives progress, informs decision-making, and shapes the future of artificial intelligence.

Importance of Data in AI

Data is the lifeblood of Artificial Intelligence (AI), serving as the foundation upon which AI systems are built, trained, and refined.

Understanding the pivotal role of data in AI is essential for comprehending the true scope and significance of this transformative technology. In this comprehensive exploration, we will delve into the importance of data in AI, highlighting how it drives innovation, informs decision-making, and shapes the future of AI.

The Role of Data in AI

At its core, AI seeks to replicate human-like intelligence and problem-solving capabilities in machines. To achieve this, AI systems require vast amounts of data, which serve several critical functions:

1. **Training AI Models:** Data is used to train AI models, providing the algorithms with examples, patterns, and information necessary to perform specific tasks. This training process is essential for enabling AI systems to recognize patterns, make predictions, and learn from experience.

2. **Testing and Validation:** Once trained, AI models need to be tested and validated to ensure their accuracy and reliability. Data is used for this purpose, allowing engineers to assess how well the AI system performs under various conditions and scenarios.

3. **Continuous Learning:** AI systems can adapt and improve over time by ingesting new data. This continuous learning process allows AI to stay relevant and effective in a rapidly changing world.

4. **Decision-Making:** In real-world applications, AI systems use data to make informed decisions. Whether it's autonomous vehicles navigating through traffic, virtual assistants providing recommendations, or healthcare AI diagnosing diseases, data plays a crucial role in the decision-making process.

5. **Generalization:** Data enables AI to generalize its knowledge. For example, if an AI model is trained on a diverse dataset of images, it can recognize new, previously unseen images that share similar characteristics to those in the training data.

Types of Data in AI

AI systems work with various types of data, each serving unique purposes in the development and operation of AI models. These data types include:

1. **Structured Data:** Structured data is highly organized and follows a predefined format. It is typically found in databases and spreadsheets and is represented in tables with rows and columns. Examples of structured data include financial records, customer information, and inventory lists. Structured data is well-suited for traditional machine learning algorithms that rely on structured input.

2. **Unstructured Data:** Unstructured data lacks a predefined structure or format, making it more complex to analyze. Examples of unstructured data include text documents, images, audio recordings, and video footage. Natural Language Processing (NLP) and Computer Vision techniques are used to extract valuable insights from unstructured data. Unstructured data is prevalent on the internet and in social media, making it a valuable source of information for AI systems.

3. **Semi-Structured Data:** Semi-structured data falls between structured and unstructured data. It may have some level of organization through tags, labels, or metadata but still offers flexibility. Common examples of semi-structured data formats include XML (eXtensible Markup Language) and JSON (JavaScript Object Notation). Semi-structured data is often encountered in web applications, data exchange formats, and NoSQL databases.

Importance of Quality Data

While data is a fundamental component of AI, the quality of the data is equally crucial. The importance of quality data in AI can be summarized as follows:

1. **Accuracy:** High-quality data ensures that AI models are trained on accurate and reliable information. Inaccurate data can lead to incorrect predictions and unreliable AI systems.

2. **Bias Mitigation:** Biases present in data can be perpetuated by AI models. Ensuring that data is free from bias and representative of diverse populations is essential for building fair and unbiased AI systems.

3. **Generalization:** Quality data allows AI models to generalize their knowledge effectively. When AI is trained on high-quality data, it can make accurate predictions and decisions in new, unseen situations.

4. **Ethical Considerations:** Ethical concerns surrounding AI, such as privacy and consent, are closely tied to the quality of data used in AI development. Ensuring that data collection and usage align with ethical standards is paramount.

Real-World Applications

The importance of data in AI is evident in its wide range of real-world applications. Here are some examples that showcase how data drives AI innovation:

1. **Healthcare:** AI is used to analyze vast amounts of medical data, including patient records, medical images, and genomic information, to assist in disease diagnosis, drug discovery, and personalized treatment plans. High-quality data is crucial for patient safety and effective healthcare delivery.

2. **Autonomous Vehicles:** Self-driving cars rely on real-time data from sensors, cameras, and GPS systems to navigate safely. These vehicles continuously process data to make split-second decisions, ensuring passenger safety and efficient transportation.

3. **E-commerce:** Recommender systems in e-commerce platforms use data on user preferences, purchase history, and browsing behavior to suggest products and personalize the shopping experience. Accurate data is essential for boosting sales and customer satisfaction.

4. **Natural Language Processing (NLP):** NLP models, such as chatbots and language translation tools, depend on linguistic data to understand and gen-

erate human language. Quality linguistic data is crucial for providing effective communication and language services.

5. **Financial Services:** AI is used to detect fraudulent transactions by analyzing vast amounts of financial data. Timely and accurate data is vital for preventing financial fraud and protecting customers' assets.

Challenges in Data Usage

While the importance of data in AI is undeniable, there are also challenges and considerations associated with data usage:

1. **Privacy:** Collecting and handling sensitive data must adhere to strict privacy regulations to protect individuals' rights and personal information. Data privacy is a critical concern in AI development.

2. **Data Security:** Safeguarding data from unauthorized access and breaches is essential. Data security measures are necessary to protect against cyber threats and data leaks.

3. **Data Bias:** Biases present in historical data can be perpetuated by AI models, leading to unfair or discriminatory outcomes. Addressing and mitigating data bias is a complex challenge.

4. **Data Volume:** In many AI applications, more data typically leads to better model performance. However, handling and processing large volumes of data require significant computational resources and storage capacity.

5. **Data Labeling:** In supervised learning scenarios, labeled data is required to train AI models. Labeling data can be a time-consuming and costly process, particularly for unstructured data.

The importance of data in AI cannot be overstated. Data serves as the foundation upon which AI systems are built, trained, and refined. It enables AI to learn, adapt, and make informed decisions in a wide range of applications, from healthcare to autonomous vehicles and e-commerce.

Different types of data, including structured, unstructured, and semi-structured data, offer unique insights and challenges for AI development. Quality data is paramount, as it ensures the accuracy, fairness, and reliability of AI systems.

As AI continues to advance, the responsible collection, handling, and usage of data will remain a central focus. Ethical considerations, privacy protection, and data security will be key concerns in the evolving landscape of AI, as we harness the power of data to drive innovation and shape the future of technology.

Fundamentals of Machine Learning

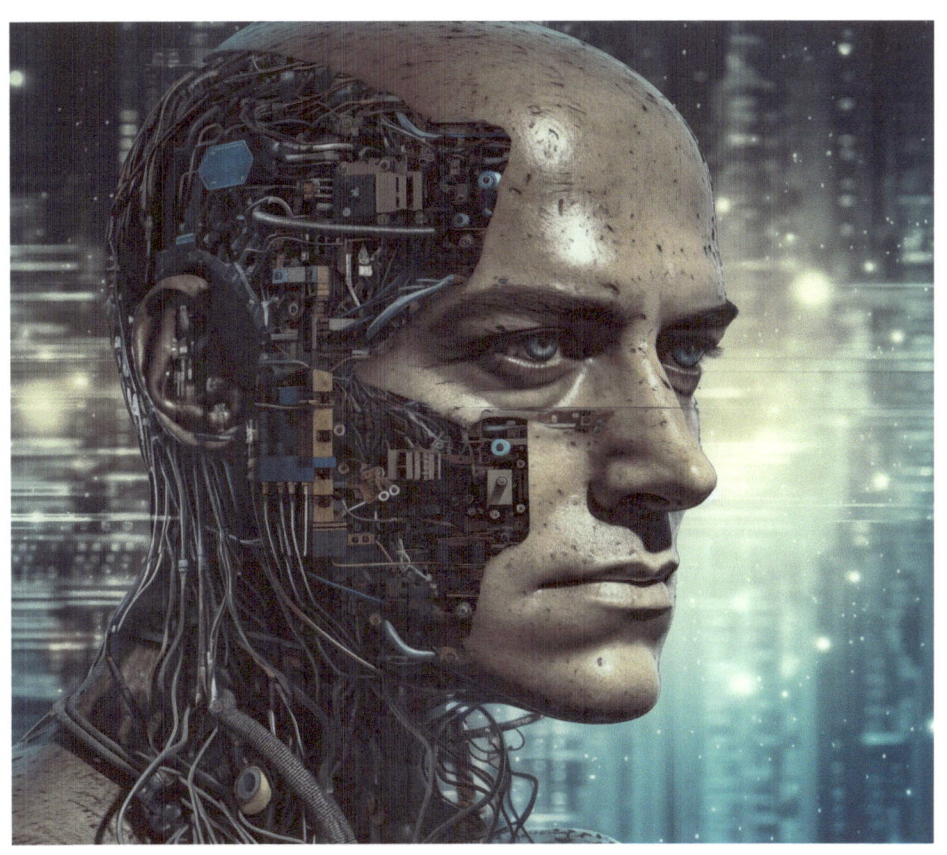

Supervised vs. Unsupervised Learning

Machine learning is a transformative field of artificial intelligence that empowers computers to learn and make decisions from data without explicit programming.

Two fundamental approaches in machine learning are Supervised Learning and Unsupervised Learning.

Understanding these approaches and their differences is essential for comprehending the core principles of machine learning.

Fundamentals of Machine Learning

Machine learning is the scientific study of algorithms and statistical models that computer systems use to perform a specific task without using explicit instructions, relying instead on patterns and inference. Here are some key fundamentals of machine learning:

1. **Data is the Foundation:** Data serves as the raw material for machine learning. Algorithms learn from data to make predictions or decisions. The quality and quantity of data significantly impact the performance of machine learning models.

2. **Learning from Experience:** Machine learning models learn from experience. They are trained on historical data, which is used to identify patterns, relationships, and trends that the model can generalize and apply to new, unseen data.

3. **Prediction and Classification:** Machine learning tasks often involve prediction and classification. For example, predicting future stock prices, classifying emails as spam or not, or identifying objects in images are common machine learning applications.

4. **Algorithm Selection:** Choosing the right algorithm for a specific task is critical. Machine learning offers a wide range of algorithms, each suitable for different types of problems. The choice of algorithm depends on the nature of the data and the desired outcome.

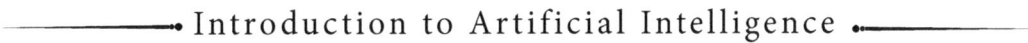
5. **Model Evaluation:** Machine learning models must be evaluated to assess their performance. Various metrics, such as accuracy, precision, recall, and F1-score, are used to measure how well a model performs on a given task.

Supervised Learning

Supervised Learning is one of the most common and well-understood paradigms in machine learning. In this approach, the algorithm learns from labeled data, where each data point is associated with the correct output or target. The goal of Supervised Learning is to learn a mapping from input data to output labels.

Key Characteristics of Supervised Learning:

1. **Labeled Data:** In Supervised Learning, the training data consists of input-output pairs, where the output (target) is known and provided for each input. For example, in a spam email classifier, the training data includes emails labeled as either spam or not spam.

2. **Goal:** The goal is to learn a model that can make accurate predictions or classifications on new, unseen data. The model should be able to generalize patterns from the training data to make correct decisions on inputs it has not encountered before.

3. **Types of Problems:** Supervised Learning is used for both regression problems (predicting continuous values, such as house prices) and classification problems (assigning data points to predefined categories, such as spam or not spam).

4. **Examples:** Common algorithms used in Supervised Learning include Linear Regression, Decision Trees, Random Forests, Support Vector Machines, and Neural Networks.

Unsupervised Learning

Unsupervised Learning, in contrast to Supervised Learning, deals with unlabeled data. In Unsupervised Learning, the algorithm is tasked with finding patterns or structure within the data without the guidance of predefined output labels. It is particularly useful for tasks like clustering and dimensionality reduction.

Key Characteristics of Unsupervised Learning:

1. **Unlabeled Data:** Unsupervised Learning operates on data where the output labels or targets are unknown. The algorithm's task is to discover hidden patterns or relationships within the data itself.

2. **Goal:** The primary goal is to explore and uncover the underlying structure in the data. This can involve grouping similar data points into clusters (clustering) or reducing the dimensionality of the data while preserving its essential characteristics (dimensionality reduction).

3. **Types of Problems:** Unsupervised Learning is commonly used for clustering tasks (grouping similar data points) and dimensionality reduction tasks (simplifying complex data by removing irrelevant features).

4. **Examples:** K-Means Clustering, Hierarchical Clustering, Principal Component Analysis (PCA), and Autoencoders are examples of algorithms used in Unsupervised Learning.

Supervised vs. Unsupervised Learning: Key Differences

1. **Label Availability:** The most significant distinction between Supervised and Unsupervised Learning is the presence of labeled data. Supervised Learning relies on labeled data, whereas Unsupervised Learning operates on unlabeled data.

2. **Goal:** Supervised Learning aims to predict or classify data based on known labels, while Unsupervised Learning seeks to uncover hidden patterns, groupings, or structures within data.

3. **Applications:** Supervised Learning is well-suited for tasks where the desired outcome is known in advance, such as image classification or language translation. Unsupervised Learning is useful for exploring data, identifying clusters in customer behavior, or reducing the dimensionality of high-dimensional data.

4. **Training:** Supervised Learning requires explicit supervision during training, as the algorithm learns to map inputs to known outputs. Unsupervised Learning relies on intrinsic properties of the data, without explicit guidance.

5. **Evaluation:** In Supervised Learning, model performance is evaluated based on its ability to make accurate predictions or classifications on labeled test data. In Unsupervised Learning, evaluation is often more challenging and relies on the quality of the discovered patterns or structures.

Real-World Applications

Both Supervised and Unsupervised Learning have a wide range of real-world applications:

Supervised Learning Applications:

1. **Speech Recognition:** Supervised learning is used to train speech recognition systems to convert spoken language into text accurately.

2. **Image Classification:** Supervised learning is employed to build image classifiers that can distinguish between different objects or scenes in images.

3. **Medical Diagnosis:** Supervised learning models can assist in diagnosing medical conditions based on patient data and medical imaging.

4. **Sentiment Analysis:** Supervised learning is used to determine sentiment in text data, such as identifying positive or negative reviews.

Unsupervised Learning Applications:

1. **Customer Segmentation:** Unsupervised learning helps businesses segment customers based on their behavior or preferences for targeted marketing.

2. **Anomaly Detection:** Unsupervised learning can identify anomalies or unusual patterns in data, such as detecting fraudulent transactions.

3. **Recommendation Systems:** Unsupervised learning techniques like collaborative filtering are used in recommendation systems to suggest products or content based on user behavior.

4. **Feature Reduction:** Dimensionality reduction techniques, such as Principal Component Analysis (PCA), are used to simplify data while preserving important information.

Supervised Learning and Unsupervised Learning are fundamental paradigms in machine learning, each with its own unique characteristics and applications. Supervised Learning relies on labeled data to make predictions or classifications, while Unsupervised Learning explores data to uncover hidden patterns or structures.

Both approaches have a profound impact on various industries, from healthcare and finance to e-commerce and natural language processing. As machine learning continues to advance, understanding when and how to apply Supervised or Unsupervised Learning is essential for leveraging the power of data-driven insights and decision-making.

Reinforcement Learning

Reinforcement Learning (RL) is a fascinating and powerful subfield of artificial intelligence (AI) that has gained increasing attention in recent years.

It is a machine learning paradigm that enables an agent to learn by interacting with an environment, making decisions to maximize a cumulative reward.

Fundamentals of Reinforcement Learning

Reinforcement Learning draws inspiration from behavioral psychology, where it mirrors the learning process observed in humans and animals as they adapt to their surroundings through trial and error.

At its core, RL involves an agent, an environment, actions, rewards, and a policy:

1. **Agent:** The agent is the learner or decision-maker, responsible for interacting with the environment and taking actions.

2. **Environment:** The environment represents the external system with which the agent interacts. It can be as simple as a game board or as complex as a physical robot navigating the real world.

3. **Actions:** Actions are the choices made by the agent to influence the environment. These actions can range from moving to a different state in a game to adjusting control parameters in a robotics application.

4. **Rewards:** Rewards are numerical values that the environment provides to the agent after each action. They serve as feedback to inform the agent about the desirability of its actions. Positive rewards encourage good decisions, while negative rewards discourage undesirable actions.

5. **Policy:** A policy is a strategy or mapping that guides the agent's decision-making. It defines the agent's behavior, specifying which action to take in each state or situation.

Key Concepts in Reinforcement Learning

To understand Reinforcement Learning more deeply, let's explore some key concepts:

1. **Markov Decision Process (MDP):** Reinforcement Learning problems are often formulated as MDPs, which consist of states, actions, transition probabilities, rewards, and a discount factor. MDPs provide a mathematical framework for modeling sequential decision-making tasks.

2. **State and Action Space:** The state space encompasses all possible states the agent can be in, while the action space includes all available actions the agent can take. The complexity of these spaces can significantly impact RL algorithms.

3. **Value Function:** The value function estimates the expected cumulative reward an agent can achieve from a given state or state-action pair. It guides the agent in making decisions that lead to higher expected rewards.

4. **Policy Optimization:** Reinforcement Learning involves optimizing the agent's policy to maximize the cumulative reward. Various methods, including Q-learning and policy gradients, are used to find the optimal policy.

5. **Exploration vs. Exploitation:** Balancing exploration (trying new actions to discover their effects) and exploitation (choosing actions known to yield high rewards) is a fundamental challenge in RL. Agents must learn to explore efficiently while exploiting learned knowledge.

Reinforcement Learning Algorithms

Reinforcement Learning offers a wide range of algorithms, each tailored to different problem domains and complexities. Some prominent RL algorithms include:

1. **Q-Learning:** Q-learning is a model-free, off-policy algorithm used for finding the optimal action-selection policy in a finite Markov decision process. It estimates the value of taking a specific action in a given state.

2. **Deep Q-Networks (DQN):** DQN is an extension of Q-learning that leverages deep neural networks to handle high-dimensional state spaces, making it suitable for applications like video games.

3. **Policy Gradients:** Policy gradient methods directly optimize the agent's policy, encouraging actions that lead to higher rewards. This approach is well-suited for problems with continuous action spaces.

4. **Actor-Critic:** Actor-critic algorithms combine elements of both policy-based and value-based methods. They feature an actor network that learns the policy and a critic network that estimates the value function.

5. **Proximal Policy Optimization (PPO):** PPO is an on-policy algorithm that addresses the problem of stability and sample efficiency in policy optimization. It has gained popularity for training complex, high-dimensional policies.

Applications of Reinforcement Learning

Reinforcement Learning has found applications in a wide range of fields, revolutionizing industries and solving complex problems. Here are some notable applications:

1. **Game Playing:** RL has excelled in game playing, with algorithms like AlphaZero mastering games like chess, Go, and Shogi through self-play and reinforcement learning.

2. **Robotics:** RL is used to train robots to perform tasks such as walking, grasping objects, and navigation in dynamic environments.

3. **Autonomous Vehicles:** Self-driving cars use RL techniques to make real-time decisions, ensuring safe and efficient navigation on roads.

4. **Healthcare:** RL assists in personalized treatment plans and drug discovery by optimizing medical interventions based on patient data.

5. **Finance:** RL is applied to algorithmic trading, portfolio optimization, and fraud detection in the financial industry.

6. **Natural Language Processing (NLP):** Chatbots and virtual assistants leverage RL for improved conversational capabilities and interaction with users.

Challenges and Considerations in Reinforcement Learning

While Reinforcement Learning has shown remarkable success in various domains, it also presents challenges and considerations:

1. **Sample Efficiency:** RL algorithms often require a large number of interactions with the environment to learn effective policies, making them data-intensive and time-consuming.

2. **Exploration Strategies:** Developing effective exploration strategies that balance the exploration of new actions with the exploitation of known policies remains a research challenge.

3. **Reward Design:** Designing appropriate reward functions is crucial, as poorly designed rewards can lead to suboptimal or unintended behavior.

4. **Safety and Ethical Concerns:** Ensuring the safety and ethical behavior of RL agents, particularly in real-world applications like autonomous vehicles, is a critical concern.

5. **Generalization:** Training RL agents to generalize from limited data to unseen scenarios is an ongoing challenge, particularly in complex environments.

Reinforcement Learning is a captivating and dynamic field of artificial intelligence that enables agents to learn through interaction with their environment, with the aim of maximizing cumulative rewards. It encompasses a rich set of concepts, algorithms, and applications that span diverse domains, from robotics and healthcare to finance and gaming.

As AI engineers and researchers continue to advance the state of the art in Reinforcement Learning, the field holds the promise of solving complex problems, making autonomous systems safer and more efficient, and pushing the boundaries of AI capabilities. Understanding the fundamentals of RL and its practical applications is key to harnessing the potential of this transformative technology.

Common Algorithms and Their Uses

Algorithms are the fundamental building blocks of computer science and play a pivotal role in solving a wide range of problems efficiently.

Understanding these algorithms and their uses is essential for anyone interested in computer science, artificial intelligence, or software development.

1. Sorting Algorithms

Sorting algorithms are essential for arranging elements in a specific order, such as ascending or descending. They are used in various applications, including data retrieval and organization.

Bubble Sort: A simple sorting algorithm that repeatedly steps through the list, compares adjacent elements, and swaps them if they are in the wrong order. It has limited practical use due to its inefficiency for large datasets.

Quick Sort: A widely used divide-and-conquer algorithm that efficiently sorts elements by selecting a 'pivot' and partitioning the array into subarrays.

Merge Sort: Another divide-and-conquer algorithm that divides the array into smaller subarrays, sorts them, and then merges them back together.

Heap Sort: A comparison-based sorting algorithm that uses a binary heap data structure to sort elements efficiently.

2. Search Algorithms

Search algorithms are used to locate specific elements within a dataset. They are fundamental in information retrieval, databases, and data analysis.

Linear Search: A simple algorithm that checks each element in a list sequentially until a match is found or the end of the list is reached.

Binary Search: An efficient algorithm used to search for an element in a sorted list by repeatedly dividing the search interval in half.

Depth-First Search (DFS): A graph traversal algorithm that explores as far as possible along one branch before backtracking.

Breadth-First Search (BFS): Another graph traversal algorithm that explores all the vertices at the current level before moving to the next level.

3. Graph Algorithms

Graph algorithms are used to analyze and manipulate graphs (collections of nodes and edges). They have applications in network design, social networks, and route planning.

Dijkstra's Algorithm: A widely used algorithm for finding the shortest path between nodes in a weighted graph, such as finding the shortest route on a map.

Floyd-Warshall Algorithm: An algorithm for finding all shortest paths between pairs of nodes in a weighted graph.

Topological Sort: Used to linearly order nodes in a directed acyclic graph (DAG). It is crucial in task scheduling and dependency resolution.

Kruskal's Algorithm: Used to find the minimum spanning tree of a connected, undirected graph. It has applications in network design and circuit layout.

4. Dynamic Programming

Dynamic programming is a technique for solving complex problems by breaking them down into smaller overlapping subproblems. It is used in various optimization and resource allocation problems.

Fibonacci Sequence: Dynamic programming can efficiently compute the nth Fibonacci number, where each number is the sum of the two preceding ones.

Longest Common Subsequence (LCS): Used in string comparison, LCS finds the longest subsequence that two sequences have in common.

Knapsack Problem: Dynamic programming is employed to determine the most valuable combination of items to include in a knapsack, given their weights and values.

Matrix Chain Multiplication: It finds the most efficient way to multiply a series of matrices, reducing the total number of multiplications required.

5. Greedy Algorithms

Greedy algorithms make locally optimal choices at each step to find a global optimum. They are used in various optimization problems where making the best choice at the moment leads to an overall optimal solution.

Dijkstra's Algorithm (Again): While Dijkstra's algorithm can be viewed as a greedy algorithm, it optimally selects the nearest unvisited node at each step to find the shortest path.

Prim's Algorithm: Used to find the minimum spanning tree of a connected, undirected graph. It selects the edge with the lowest weight at each step.

Huffman Coding: Greedy algorithm for lossless data compression, where the most frequent characters are assigned shorter binary codes.

Fractional Knapsack Problem: A greedy algorithm is used to maximize the total value of items placed in a knapsack while respecting its weight capacity.

Machine Learning Algorithms

Machine learning algorithms are essential in artificial intelligence for tasks like classification, regression, clustering, and pattern recognition.

Linear Regression: Used for predicting a continuous outcome variable (dependent variable) based on one or more predictor variables (independent variables).

Decision Trees: Tree-based algorithms that recursively split data into subsets based on the most significant attribute, used for both classification and regression.

K-Means Clustering: Unsupervised learning algorithm that partitions data points into clusters based on similarity.

Support Vector Machines (SVM): A powerful algorithm used for classification tasks by finding an optimal hyperplane that separates data points into different classes.

Random Forest: Ensemble learning method that combines multiple decision trees to improve predictive accuracy and reduce overfitting.

7. Cryptography Algorithms

Cryptography algorithms are essential for securing data and communication in various applications, including online banking and e-commerce.

RSA Algorithm: Widely used for secure data transmission and digital signatures, based on the mathematical properties of large prime numbers.

AES (Advanced Encryption Standard): Symmetric-key encryption algorithm used for encrypting and decrypting data securely.

Diffie-Hellman Key Exchange: A cryptographic protocol used to secure the exchange of keys for secure communication over public channels.

Elliptic Curve Cryptography (ECC): An encryption technique based on elliptic curves, known for its efficiency and security.

8. Neural Network Algorithms

Neural networks are the building blocks of deep learning and have applications in image and speech recognition, natural language processing, and more.

Feedforward Neural Networks (FNN): Basic neural network architecture for tasks like image classification and regression.

Convolutional Neural Networks (CNN): Specialized neural networks for image and video analysis, known for their ability to learn spatial hierarchies of features.

Recurrent Neural Networks (RNN): Designed for sequence data, RNNs have applications in speech recognition, language modeling, and time series analysis.

Long Short-Term Memory (LSTM): A type of RNN designed to handle long sequences and mitigate the vanishing gradient problem.

Applications of These Algorithms

Common algorithms find applications in various domains and industries, including:

1. **Computer Science and Software Engineering:** Algorithms are the foundation of software development, used in data structures, sorting, searching, and optimization.

2. **Data Analysis and Statistics:** Algorithms like regression and clustering are employed to extract insights from data.

3. **Artificial Intelligence and Machine Learning:** Algorithms enable AI systems to learn from data and make predictions or decisions.

4. **Finance:** Algorithms are used in trading strategies, risk assessment, and portfolio optimization.

5. **Networking:** Graph algorithms play a crucial role in network design

Neural Networks and Deep Learning

Basics of Neural Networks

Neural networks are at the heart of modern artificial intelligence, revolutionizing fields like computer vision, natural language processing, and robotics.

These versatile computational models, inspired by the human brain, have become essential tools for solving complex problems, making predictions, and recognizing patterns in data.

Definition of a Neural Network

A neural network is a computational model consisting of interconnected processing units, inspired by the structure and function of biological neurons in the human brain.

These interconnected units, also called artificial neurons or nodes, work together to process and learn from data.

Basic Components of a Neural Network

To understand how neural networks operate, let's break down their essential components:

1. **Input Layer:** The input layer receives data, which can be in various forms, such as images, text, or numerical values. Each neuron in the input layer corresponds to a feature or element of the input data.

2. **Hidden Layers:** Between the input and output layers, neural networks can have one or more hidden layers. These layers perform the bulk of the computation in the network and are responsible for learning and representing complex patterns in the data.

3. **Output Layer:** The output layer produces the final results or predictions based on the information processed in the hidden layers. The number of

neurons in the output layer depends on the nature of the task (e.g., classification, regression).

4. **Weights:** Each connection between neurons has a weight associated with it. These weights determine the strength of the connection and are adjusted during training to optimize the network's performance.

5. **Activation Functions:** Activation functions introduce non-linearity to the neural network, allowing it to model complex relationships in the data. Common activation functions include the sigmoid, ReLU (Rectified Linear Unit), and tanh (hyperbolic tangent) functions.

How Neural Networks Work

The operation of a neural network can be broken down into several steps:

1. **Input:** The input layer receives the initial data, whether it's an image's pixel values, words in a text, or numerical features.

2. **Weighted Sum:** Each neuron in the hidden layers computes a weighted sum of its inputs, where the weights represent the strength of the connections. This weighted sum is then passed through an activation function.

3. **Activation Function:** The activation function introduces non-linearity to the model, allowing it to capture complex patterns and relationships in the data. For example, the ReLU activation function returns the input if it's positive and zero otherwise.

4. **Forward Propagation:** The computed values and activations are propagated forward through the network from the input layer to the output layer. This process is known as forward propagation.

5. **Output:** The output layer produces the final results or predictions based on the processed data.

Training a Neural Network

The strength of neural networks lies in their ability to learn from data through a process called training. Training involves the following steps:

1. **Initialization:** Initially, the weights of the network are assigned random values.

2. **Forward Propagation:** Training data is passed through the network, and predictions are made. These predictions are compared to the actual target values.

3. **Loss Calculation:** A loss function measures the error or difference between the predicted values and the actual targets. Common loss functions include mean squared error for regression tasks and cross-entropy loss for classification tasks.

4. **Backpropagation:** The calculated loss is propagated backward through the network using a technique called backpropagation. This involves computing the gradients of the loss with respect to the weights.

5. **Weight Update:** The weights of the network are updated using optimization algorithms like gradient descent. These updates aim to minimize the loss and improve the network's performance.

6. **Iterative Process:** Steps 2 to 5 are repeated iteratively, adjusting the weights to minimize the loss. This process continues until the network converges to a solution or reaches a predefined stopping criterion.

Types of Neural Networks

Neural networks come in various architectures and configurations, each designed for specific tasks. Some common types of neural networks include:

1. **Feedforward Neural Networks (FNN):** These networks have a simple architecture with layers of neurons connected in a feedforward manner. They are used for tasks like regression and binary classification.

2. **Convolutional Neural Networks (CNN):** CNNs are specialized for image and video processing tasks. They use convolutional layers to automatically extract features from visual data.

3. **Recurrent Neural Networks (RNN):** RNNs are designed for sequence data, making them suitable for tasks like natural language processing and time series analysis. They have recurrent connections that allow information to persist through time steps.

4. **Long Short-Term Memory (LSTM):** A variation of RNNs, LSTMs address the vanishing gradient problem by allowing the network to learn long-range dependencies in sequences.

5. **Generative Adversarial Networks (GAN):** GANs consist of a generator and a discriminator that compete against each other. They are used for tasks like image generation and data augmentation.

6. **Autoencoders:** Autoencoders are used for dimensionality reduction and feature learning. They consist of an encoder and a decoder that aim to reconstruct the input data.

Applications of Neural Networks

Neural networks have found applications in various fields and domains:

1. **Computer Vision:** CNNs are used for image recognition, object detection, and facial recognition.

2. **Natural Language Processing (NLP):** RNNs and transformers are used for tasks like machine translation, sentiment analysis, and chatbots.

3. **Healthcare:** Neural networks assist in medical image analysis, disease diagnosis, and drug discovery.

4. **Autonomous Vehicles:** CNNs and reinforcement learning are employed for self-driving cars to process sensor data and make driving decisions.

5. **Finance:** Neural networks are used for fraud detection, stock market prediction, and algorithmic trading.

6. **Gaming:** Neural networks play a significant role in game development for character animation, game testing, and AI opponents.

7. **Recommendation Systems:** Collaborative filtering and deep learning are used to provide personalized recommendations on platforms like Netflix and Amazon.

Challenges and Considerations

While neural networks have achieved remarkable success, they come with challenges and considerations:

1. **Data Quality:** Neural networks require large and high-quality datasets for training. Poor or biased data can lead to biased models.

2. **Overfitting:** Neural networks are prone to overfitting, where they memorize the training data but perform poorly on unseen data. Techniques like regularization are used to mitigate this issue.

3. **Computational Resources:** Training deep neural networks requires significant computational resources, including powerful GPUs and TPUs.

4. **Interpretability:** Neural networks are often considered black-box models, making it challenging to interpret their decisions and reasoning.

5. **Ethical Concerns:** The use of neural networks in applications like surveillance and decision-making raises ethical concerns related to privacy, bias, and fairness.

Neural networks are a cornerstone of modern artificial intelligence, enabling machines to learn from data and make intelligent decisions.

Their versatility and ability to model complex patterns have led to groundbreaking advancements in various fields, from computer vision and natural language processing to healthcare and finance.

Understanding the basics of neural networks is essential for anyone interested in AI, machine learning, or data science, as they continue to shape the future of technology and innovation.

Introduction to Deep Learning

Deep learning is a revolutionary subfield of artificial intelligence (AI) that has reshaped the landscape of machine learning and enabled breakthroughs in various domains such as computer vision, natural language processing, and robotics.

What is Deep Learning?

Deep learning is a subset of machine learning that focuses on training artificial neural networks to learn and make decisions in a manner that mimics the human brain. At its core, deep learning leverages deep neural networks, which are composed of multiple layers of interconnected artificial neurons. These networks can automatically discover and represent complex patterns and relationships within data, making them exceptionally powerful for tasks such as image recognition, speech synthesis, and language translation.

Key Components of Deep Learning

To grasp the fundamentals of deep learning, it's essential to understand its key components:

1. **Artificial Neurons (Nodes):** These are the basic building blocks of deep neural networks. Artificial neurons receive inputs, apply mathematical operations, and produce outputs. Each neuron is akin to a simple computational unit that can model the behavior of biological neurons.

2. **Layers:** Deep neural networks consist of multiple layers, typically categorized as input, hidden, and output layers. The depth of the network is what makes it "deep." Input layers receive data, hidden layers process it, and output layers produce results.

3. **Weights and Biases:** Weights and biases are parameters associated with the connections between neurons. Weights determine the strength of connections, while biases introduce flexibility in the neuron's activation function.

4. **Activation Functions:** Activation functions introduce non-linearity into the network, allowing it to model complex relationships in data. Common activation functions include the sigmoid, ReLU (Rectified Linear Unit), and tanh functions.

5. **Loss Function:** The loss function quantifies the error or difference between the network's predictions and the actual target values. The goal during training is to minimize this loss.

6. **Optimization Algorithms:** Optimization algorithms, such as gradient descent, are used to update weights and biases during training to minimize the loss function gradually.

7. **Backpropagation:** Backpropagation is a critical algorithm for training deep neural networks. It calculates the gradients of the loss function with respect to the network's weights and biases, enabling weight updates that improve the network's performance.

How Deep Learning Works

Deep learning operates through a sequence of steps, which can be summarized as follows:

1. **Initialization:** Initially, the weights and biases of the neural network are assigned random values.

2. **Forward Propagation:** Training data is fed into the network, and predictions are made by passing the data through the layers. This process is known as forward propagation.

3. **Loss Calculation:** A loss function measures the error between the predicted values and the actual targets. This error is used to quantify how well the network is performing.

4. **Backpropagation:** The calculated loss is propagated backward through the network using backpropagation. This process involves computing gradients that indicate how the weights and biases should be adjusted to minimize the loss.

5. **Weight Update:** Optimization algorithms like gradient descent are employed to update the network's weights and biases iteratively. These updates aim to reduce the loss, improving the network's predictive accuracy.

6. **Iterative Process:** Steps 2 to 5 are repeated iteratively for a fixed number of epochs or until the network converges to a satisfactory solution.

Deep Learning Architectures

Deep learning offers various architectural configurations tailored to specific tasks:

1. Feedforward Neural Networks (FNN): These networks consist of layers of neurons connected in a feedforward manner. They are suitable for tasks like regression and binary classification.

2. **Convolutional Neural Networks (CNN):** CNNs are specialized for image and video processing tasks. They use convolutional layers to automatically extract features from visual data.

3. **Recurrent Neural Networks (RNN):** RNNs are designed for sequence data, making them ideal for tasks like natural language processing and time series analysis. They have recurrent connections that allow information to persist through time steps.

4. **Long Short-Term Memory (LSTM):** LSTMs are a variation of RNNs that address the vanishing gradient problem, enabling the network to learn long-range dependencies in sequences.

5. **Generative Adversarial Networks (GAN):** GANs consist of a generator and a discriminator that compete against each other. They are used for tasks like image generation and data augmentation.

6. **Autoencoders:** Autoencoders are employed for dimensionality reduction and feature learning. They consist of an encoder and a decoder that aim to reconstruct the input data.

Applications of Deep Learning

Deep learning has made significant contributions to various fields and domains:

1. **Computer Vision:** CNNs are used for image recognition, object detection, and facial recognition in applications like self-driving cars and security systems.

2. **Natural Language Processing (NLP):** RNNs and transformers are employed for machine translation, sentiment analysis, chatbots, and speech recognition.

3. **Healthcare:** Deep learning assists in medical image analysis, disease diagnosis, drug discovery, and personalized treatment plans.

4. **Autonomous Vehicles:** CNNs and reinforcement learning are used for processing sensor data and making driving decisions in self-driving cars.

5. **Finance:** Deep learning models are utilized for fraud detection, stock market prediction, algorithmic trading, and risk assessment.

6. **Gaming:** Deep reinforcement learning is applied in game development for character animation, game testing, and creating intelligent AI opponents.

7. **Recommendation Systems:** Collaborative filtering and deep learning techniques provide personalized recommendations on platforms like Netflix and Amazon.

Challenges and Considerations

While deep learning has achieved remarkable success, it comes with challenges and considerations:

1. **Data Quality:** Deep learning models require large and high-quality datasets for training. Poor or biased data can lead to biased models.

2. **Overfitting:** Deep neural networks are prone to overfitting, where they memorize the training data but perform poorly on unseen data. Techniques like regularization are used to mitigate this issue.

3. **Computational Resources:** Training deep neural networks requires significant computational resources, including powerful GPUs and TPUs.

4. **Interpretability:** Deep learning models are often considered black-box models, making it challenging to interpret their decisions and reasoning.

5. **Ethical Concerns:** The use of deep learning in applications like surveillance and decision-making raises ethical concerns related to privacy, bias, and fairness.

Deep learning represents a paradigm shift in artificial intelligence, enabling machines to learn complex patterns and make intelligent decisions. Its applications span a wide range of fields, from computer vision and natural language processing to healthcare and finance. Understanding the basics of deep learning is essential for anyone interested in AI, machine learning, or data science, as it continues to drive innovation and shape the future of technology.

Convolutional Neural Networks (CNNs) and Recurrent Neural Networks (RNNs)

Introduction

In the ever-evolving landscape of artificial intelligence (AI) and deep learning, Convolutional Neural Networks (CNNs) and Recurrent Neural Networks (RNNs) stand as two of the most influential and widely used architectural innovations.

These neural network variants are tailored to address specific challenges and excel in various domains.

Convolutional Neural Networks (CNNs)

CNNs are a class of deep neural networks primarily designed for tasks involving structured grid-like data, with a particular focus on computer vision applications. The innovation that sets CNNs apart from traditional neural networks is the convolution operation.

Key Components of CNNs

1. **Convolutional Layers:** These layers apply convolution operations to input data. Convolution involves sliding a small filter (also known as a kernel) over the input data to detect patterns and features. Each filter learns to recognize specific features like edges, textures, or shapes.

2. **Pooling Layers:** Pooling layers downsample the spatial dimensions of the feature maps generated by convolutional layers. Max-pooling and average-pooling are common pooling operations that help reduce computational complexity and retain essential information.

3. **Activation Functions:** CNNs typically use non-linear activation functions like ReLU (Rectified Linear Unit) to introduce non-linearity into the model, enabling it to learn complex patterns.

4. **Fully Connected Layers:** After feature extraction and reduction, CNNs often employ one or more fully connected layers, similar to traditional neural networks, to perform classification or regression tasks.

How CNNs Work

The operation of CNNs can be summarized in several steps:

1. **Convolution:** Convolutional layers apply convolution operations to the input data, creating feature maps that highlight important patterns.
2. **Activation:** Activation functions are applied to the feature maps, introducing non-linearity.
3. **Pooling:** Pooling layers downsample the feature maps by selecting the most important values, reducing computational demands.
4. **Flattening:** The pooled feature maps are flattened into a one-dimensional vector.
5. **Fully Connected Layers:** The flattened vector is passed through one or more fully connected layers for classification or regression.
6. **Output:** The final layer produces predictions or classifications based on the learned features.

Applications of CNNs

CNNs have made significant contributions to various fields, with applications including:

1. **Image Classification:** CNNs excel in classifying images into predefined categories, making them the foundation of modern computer vision.
2. **Object Detection:** CNNs are used in object detection tasks, locating and classifying objects within images or video frames.
3. **Image Segmentation:** They help segment images into distinct regions, aiding in tasks like medical image analysis and autonomous navigation.

4. **Face Recognition**: CNNs are employed in face recognition systems for security and authentication purposes.

5. **Natural Language Processing (NLP):** CNNs are used for text classification, sentiment analysis, and document categorization in NLP tasks.

6. **Autonomous Vehicles:** CNNs process sensor data, including camera feeds, in self-driving cars for object detection and scene analysis.

Recurrent Neural Networks (RNNs)

RNNs are a class of neural networks well-suited for tasks that involve sequences of data, such as time series, natural language, and speech. Unlike traditional feedforward networks, RNNs have loops, allowing them to maintain a hidden state that captures information from previous time steps.

Key Components of RNNs

1. **Hidden State:** RNNs maintain a hidden state that represents the network's memory or context. This hidden state is updated at each time step and carries information from previous steps.

2. **Recurrent Connections:** The recurrent connections in RNNs enable them to pass information from one time step to the next, allowing the network to process sequences of data.

3. **Input Data:** RNNs receive input data at each time step, which can vary in dimensionality, such as word embeddings in natural language processing or sensor readings in time series analysis.

4. **Output:** RNNs produce an output at each time step, and the final output is often used for prediction or classification.

How RNNs Work

The operation of RNNs can be broken down into several steps:

1. **Initialization:** The hidden state is initialized to zeros or small random values.

2. **Input Processing:** The network receives input data at each time step, which is combined with the previous hidden state to update the current hidden state.

3. **Hidden State Update:** The updated hidden state retains information from previous time steps, serving as the network's memory.

4. **Output Generation:** RNNs produce an output at each time step, which can be used for prediction, classification, or generating sequences.

5. **Sequence Length:** The network processes data for a fixed number of time steps or until the sequence ends.

Challenges of RNNs

Traditional RNNs suffer from certain limitations:

1. **Vanishing Gradient:** RNNs can struggle to capture long-range dependencies in sequences due to the vanishing gradient problem. This can lead to difficulties in learning and modeling.

2. **Lack of Parallelism:** RNNs process sequences sequentially, limiting their parallelism and potentially slowing down training.

LSTM and GRU

To address the vanishing gradient problem, variations of RNNs have been developed, including Long Short-Term Memory (LSTM) and Gated Recurrent Unit (GRU).

1. **LSTM:** LSTMs introduce a gating mechanism that allows the network to learn when to forget or remember information. This makes them particularly effective at capturing long-term dependencies.

2. **GRU:** GRUs are similar to LSTMs but have a simplified architecture with fewer gates. They strike a balance between performance and simplicity.

Applications of RNNs

RNNs have found applications in numerous fields, including:

1. **Natural Language Processing:** RNNs are used for tasks like language modeling, text generation, machine translation, and speech recognition.
2. **Time Series Analysis:** They excel in time series forecasting, stock market prediction, and anomaly detection.
3. **Autonomous Vehicles**: RNNs process sensor data, including lidar and radar, to make real-time driving decisions.
4. **Healthcare:** RNNs analyze patient data for early disease detection and patient monitoring.
5. **Financial Forecasting:** They are applied in stock market prediction, algorithmic trading, and risk assessment.
6. **Robotics:** RNNs control robotic systems for tasks such as object manipulation and autonomous navigation.

CNNs vs. RNNs

While CNNs and RNNs serve distinct purposes, they can also complement each other in certain applications:

1. **Image Captioning:** Combining CNNs and RNNs allows for generating descriptive captions for images, where CNNs extract image features, and RNNs generate natural language descriptions.
2. **Video Analysis:** CNNs can extract spatial features from video frames, while RNNs can model temporal dependencies between frames, enabling action recognition and video captioning.
3. **Speech Recognition:** CNNs are used for feature extraction from audio spectrograms, while RNNs process sequences of features to transcribe speech.

4. **Neural Machine Translation:** A combination of CNNs and RNNs has led to significant advancements in machine translation, where CNNs encode source language sentences, and RNNs generate target language translations.

Convolutional Neural Networks (CNNs) and Recurrent Neural Networks (RNNs) are powerful neural network architectures that have reshaped the landscape of deep learning. CNNs excel in structured grid-like data, making them ideal for computer vision tasks, while RNNs are tailored for sequential data and find applications in natural language processing and time series analysis. Both CNNs and RNNs have evolved to address challenges and limitations, with variants like LSTM and GRU improving their effectiveness. Understanding the strengths and applications of CNNs and RNNs is essential for anyone working in AI, as they continue to drive innovation in a wide range of fields.

Natural Language Processing (NLP)

Understanding Language and Text in AI

Natural Language Processing (NLP) is a fascinating and dynamic field of artificial intelligence (AI) that focuses on enabling computers to understand, interpret, and generate human language.

With applications spanning from chatbots and machine translation to sentiment analysis and content recommendation, NLP plays a pivotal role in our daily lives.

What is Natural Language Processing (NLP)?

NLP is a subfield of AI that combines computer science, linguistics, and machine learning to empower machines to comprehend, process, and generate human language.

It seeks to bridge the gap between the complex nuances of human communication and the capabilities of computers.

Key Components of NLP

To understand the inner workings of NLP, let's break down its key components:

1. **Text Data:** NLP primarily deals with text data, which can be in the form of written documents, transcripts, social media posts, or any other textual content.
2. **Tokenization:** Tokenization is the process of breaking down text into individual units, or tokens. Tokens can be words, phrases, or even characters, depending on the level of granularity required.
3. **Language Understanding:** NLP algorithms aim to understand the structure and meaning of language, including grammar, syntax, semantics, and context.

4. **Machine Learning:** Machine learning techniques, such as deep learning and natural language models, are employed to train NLP systems to recognize patterns and make predictions.

5. **Natural Language Generation:** NLP also involves generating human-like text, which is particularly useful in chatbots, content creation, and automated report generation.

How NLP Works

The functioning of NLP can be summarized in several steps:

1. **Text Preprocessing:** Raw text data is preprocessed to remove noise, such as punctuation and special characters. Tokenization breaks text into manageable units.

2. **Feature Extraction:** Features are extracted from the text, such as word frequencies, word embeddings (vector representations of words), and syntactic structures.

3. **Machine Learning Models:** NLP models, often based on deep learning architectures like transformers, are trained on labeled data to learn patterns and relationships in the text.

4. **Predictions and Analysis:** Trained models can be used to make predictions, classify text into categories, perform sentiment analysis, or generate human-like responses.

5. **Feedback Loop:** NLP systems can improve over time through a feedback loop where user interactions and feedback are used to refine the model's performance.

Applications of NLP

NLP has permeated various industries and applications, including:

1. **Chatbots and Virtual Assistants:** Chatbots use NLP to understand and respond to user queries, making them valuable in customer support and service industries.

2. **Machine Translation:** NLP powers machine translation systems like Google Translate, breaking down language barriers for global communication.

3. **Sentiment Analysis:** Businesses use NLP to analyze customer sentiment from social media, reviews, and surveys to inform decision-making.

4. **Information Retrieval:** Search engines like Google utilize NLP to provide relevant search results based on user queries.

5. **Speech Recognition:** NLP enables voice assistants like Siri and Alexa to understand and respond to spoken commands.

6. **Text Summarization:** NLP is used to automatically generate summaries of lengthy texts, making information more digestible.

7. **Language Generation:** Content generation tools rely on NLP to produce human-like articles, reports, and creative writing.

8. **Medical Diagnosis:** NLP assists in extracting information from medical records and clinical reports for diagnosis and research.

Challenges in NLP

Despite its advancements, NLP faces several challenges:

1. **Ambiguity:** Language is inherently ambiguous, making it challenging for machines to interpret context and meaning accurately.

2. **Idioms and Slang:** Language evolves rapidly, introducing idioms, slang, and cultural references that can be perplexing for NLP models.

3. **Multilingualism:** NLP must address the complexities of multiple languages, dialects, and regional variations.

4. **Lack of Data:** Training NLP models requires vast amounts of annotated data, which can be scarce for less commonly spoken languages or specialized domains.

5. **Bias and Fairness:** NLP models can inherit biases present in training data, leading to unfair or biased results, particularly in areas like gender or ethnicity.

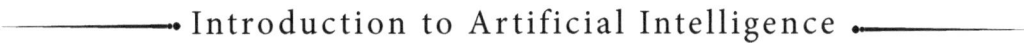

State-of-the-Art NLP Models

Recent advancements in NLP have been driven by state-of-the-art models like GPT (Generative Pre-trained Transformer) and BERT (Bidirectional Encoder Representations from Transformers). These models have demonstrated remarkable language understanding and generation capabilities and have been pre-trained on large-scale text corpora to capture intricate language nuances.

GPT-3 (Generative Pre-trained Transformer 3): Developed by OpenAI, GPT-3 is one of the largest and most powerful NLP models. It has been used for tasks like text completion, content generation, and language translation.

BERT (Bidirectional Encoder Representations from Transformers): BERT, developed by Google AI, introduced a bidirectional context understanding approach. It has significantly improved the accuracy of NLP models in various tasks, including question answering and sentiment analysis.

Ethical Considerations

NLP's power to analyze and generate text comes with ethical responsibilities:

1. **Bias Mitigation:** Developers must actively work to reduce biases in NLP models to ensure fairness and equity in applications.
2. **Privacy Concerns:** NLP systems should adhere to privacy regulations and handle personal data with care.
3. **Misinformation and Deepfakes:** NLP's capacity to generate convincing text raises concerns about the spread of misinformation and deepfake content.
4. **Accessibility:** Efforts should be made to ensure NLP technologies are accessible to all, including those with disabilities.

The Future of NLP

The field of NLP continues to evolve rapidly, with exciting developments on the horizon:

1. **Multimodal NLP:** Combining NLP with computer vision and audio processing to understand and generate text from multiple modalities.

2. **Zero-shot Learning:** Advancements in zero-shot learning aim to enable NLP models to perform tasks with little or no training data.

3. **Conversational AI:** The development of more human-like chatbots and virtual assistants that can engage in complex conversations.

4. **Explainable AI:** Efforts to make NLP models more transparent and interpretable, addressing the "black-box" nature of deep learning.

5. **Cross-lingual Understanding:** Improving NLP models' ability to handle multiple languages seamlessly.

Natural Language Processing (NLP) represents an exciting and rapidly advancing field within artificial intelligence, with applications that touch nearly every aspect of our lives. Its ability to understand and generate human language is transforming industries, from customer service and healthcare to content creation and language translation. As NLP continues to evolve, it brings both immense possibilities and ethical challenges.

Understanding the fundamentals of NLP is essential for anyone interested in AI, data science, or the future of human-computer interaction.

Sentiment Analysis, Chatbots, and Translation: AI Transforming Communication

In today's digital age, artificial intelligence (AI) has ushered in transformative changes in the way we communicate.

This includes our ability to understand and analyze sentiments, interact with chatbots, and bridge language barriers through translation.

Sentiment Analysis

Sentiment analysis, also known as opinion mining, is an AI-driven technique that focuses on understanding and extracting emotions, opinions, and attitudes expressed in text data.

It holds immense value for businesses, marketers, and researchers to gauge public sentiment, customer satisfaction, and brand perception.

Key Components of Sentiment Analysis

To comprehend sentiment analysis, it's important to understand its key components:

1. **Text Data:** Sentiment analysis primarily deals with text data, including social media posts, product reviews, customer feedback, and news articles.

2. **Text Preprocessing:** Raw text data is preprocessed to remove irrelevant information, such as punctuation and special characters. Tokenization divides the text into individual words or phrases.

3. **Sentiment Classification:** Sentiment analysis models classify text into predefined categories, typically positive, negative, or neutral. More advanced models can distinguish finer-grained emotions.

4. **Machine Learning Models:** Machine learning algorithms, including natural language processing (NLP) models like recurrent neural networks (RNNs)

and transformers, are trained on labeled data to recognize patterns associated with sentiments.

5. **Sentiment Scores:** Sentiment scores quantify the degree of positivity or negativity in text, providing a numerical measure of sentiment strength.

How Sentiment Analysis Works

The process of sentiment analysis involves several steps:

1. **Data Collection:** Text data is collected from various sources, such as social media platforms, customer reviews, or surveys.

2. **Text Preprocessing:** Data preprocessing ensures that the text is clean and ready for analysis, including tasks like lowercasing, tokenization, and stemming (reducing words to their base form).

3. **Sentiment Classification:** Machine learning models are trained on labeled data, where text samples are categorized as positive, negative, or neutral sentiments.

4. **Prediction:** The trained model is applied to new, unlabeled data to classify it into sentiment categories.

5. **Sentiment Scores:** Sentiment analysis tools often provide sentiment scores, which indicate the strength and polarity (positive or negative) of sentiment in text.

Applications of Sentiment Analysis

Sentiment analysis has diverse applications, including:

1. **Brand Monitoring:** Companies use sentiment analysis to monitor brand perception and customer sentiment on social media.

2. **Customer Support:** Sentiment analysis helps identify customer dissatisfaction and provides insights for improving support services.

3. **Market Research:** Businesses can gauge market sentiment and make data-driven decisions for product development and marketing campaigns.

4. **Political Analysis:** Sentiment analysis is used to understand public opinion during elections and political events.

5. **Product Reviews:** E-commerce platforms utilize sentiment analysis to summarize and categorize product reviews.

Chatbots

Chatbots, or conversational agents, are AI-driven systems designed to interact with users in a human-like manner through text or speech. They have gained prominence in customer service, virtual assistants, and various automated communication scenarios.

Key Components of Chatbots

To understand chatbots, let's break down their key components:

1. **User Interface:** Chatbots interact with users through text-based interfaces, such as messaging apps, websites, or voice assistants.

2. **Natural Language Processing (NLP):** NLP is at the core of chatbots, enabling them to understand and generate human language. It involves tasks like text recognition, intent identification, and response generation.

3. **Dialog Management:** Chatbots employ dialog management techniques to maintain context, handle user requests, and provide relevant responses in a conversational flow.

4. **Knowledge Base:** Chatbots may access a knowledge base or database to retrieve information and answer user queries accurately.

How Chatbots Work

The operation of chatbots can be summarized in several steps:

1. **User Input:** Chatbots receive user input in the form of text or voice commands.

2. **Intent Recognition:** NLP models analyze user input to determine the user's intent or request.

3. **Dialog Management:** The chatbot maintains context and engages in a conversation, following predefined dialog flows or decision trees.

4. **Response Generation:** Based on the user's intent and context, the chatbot generates a response, which is delivered to the user.

5. **Iterative Interaction:** Chatbots can engage in back-and-forth interactions with users to fulfill requests, provide information, or assist with tasks.

Applications of Chatbots

Chatbots find application in various domains, including:

1. **Customer Service:** Chatbots handle customer inquiries, provide support, and assist with common issues.

2. **Virtual Assistants:** Voice-activated chatbots like Siri and Alexa assist users with tasks, inquiries, and home automation.

3. **E-commerce:** Chatbots help users navigate e-commerce platforms, answer product questions, and facilitate purchases.

4. **Healthcare:** Healthcare chatbots offer medical advice, appointment scheduling, and symptom assessment.

5. **Education:** Chatbots aid in online learning, answering student queries and providing tutoring.

Translation

Translation, in the context of AI, refers to the automatic conversion of text or speech from one language to another. AI-driven translation models have revolutionized language communication and content accessibility across borders.

Key Components of Translation

Understanding translation involves recognizing its key components:

1. **Source Language:** The original text or speech that needs to be translated.
2. **Target Language:** The language into which the source content is to be translated.
3. **Parallel Corpora:** Bilingual or multilingual datasets used for training translation models.
4. **Neural Machine Translation (NMT):** Modern translation models, often based on neural networks, that excel in capturing context and producing fluent translations.

How Translation Works

The translation process encompasses several steps:

1. **Text Segmentation:** Text is divided into sentences or phrases to facilitate translation.
2. **Neural Model Training:** Translation models are trained on parallel corpora, learning to map text from the source language to the target language.
3. **Inference:** When a user inputs text in the source language, the trained model generates a translation in the target language.
4. **Post-Editing:** Depending on the quality and context of the translation, post-editing may be necessary for refinement.

Applications of Translation

Translation technology is pervasive in today's globalized world, with applications including:

1. **Cross-Language Communication:** Translation enables people from different linguistic backgrounds to communicate effectively.
2. **Content Localization:** Businesses use translation to adapt their content for international markets.
3. **Multilingual Content Creation:** Writers and content creators use translation tools for multilingual content production.

4. **Language Learning:** Translation aids language learners in understanding and practicing new languages.

5. **Travel and Tourism:** Translation apps help travelers navigate foreign countries and communicate with locals.

Sentiment analysis, chatbots, and translation represent three AI-driven pillars of modern communication. Sentiment analysis provides insights into human emotions and opinions, enabling informed decision-making. Chatbots facilitate human-computer interactions, enhancing customer service and user engagement. Translation technology breaks down language barriers, fostering global communication and accessibility.

As AI continues to advance, these communication technologies will become increasingly sophisticated and integral to our daily lives. Understanding their fundamentals is essential for anyone interested in AI, technology, or the future of human-computer interaction.

Computer Vision

Image Recognition and Object Detection: AI's Visionary Capabilities

In the realm of artificial intelligence (AI), image recognition and object detection stand as remarkable achievements.

These technologies have revolutionized the way machines perceive and interact with the visual world.

Image Recognition

Image recognition, also known as image classification, is the process of training a computer to identify and categorize objects or patterns within an image.

It allows machines to understand and interpret visual data, making it a pivotal component of AI applications involving images.

Key Components of Image Recognition

To comprehend image recognition, it's important to understand its key components:

1. **Image Data:** Image recognition primarily deals with image data, which can range from photographs and illustrations to medical scans and satellite imagery.
2. **Convolutional Neural Networks (CNNs):** CNNs are the backbone of image recognition models. They consist of layers of convolutional and pooling operations that extract features from images.
3. **Training Data:** Image recognition models are trained on labeled datasets, where images are associated with corresponding categories or labels.
4. **Machine Learning:** Supervised machine learning techniques are employed to train image recognition models to recognize patterns and features within images.

5. **Classifiers:** Image recognition models use classifiers to assign images to predefined categories or labels based on the features detected.

How Image Recognition Works

The process of image recognition can be summarized in several steps:

1. **Data Collection:** A dataset containing images and corresponding labels is collected and prepared for training.

2. **Data Preprocessing:** Image data is preprocessed to standardize size, format, and quality.

3. **Feature Extraction:** CNNs analyze images to extract features, such as edges, textures, and shapes.

4. **Training:** The model is trained on the labeled dataset, learning to associate image features with categories or labels.

5. **Prediction:** When presented with a new image, the trained model analyzes it, extracts features, and assigns it to the most appropriate category.

Applications of Image Recognition

Image recognition has found applications across various domains, including:

1. **Healthcare:** Image recognition aids in medical diagnosis, detecting diseases from medical images like X-rays and MRIs.

2. **Autonomous Vehicles:** Self-driving cars use image recognition to identify and navigate around objects, pedestrians, and road signs.

3. **Agriculture:** Image recognition is used in precision agriculture to monitor crop health and identify pests or diseases.

4. **E-commerce:** Online retailers employ image recognition for product recommendation and visual search.

5. **Security:** Surveillance systems use image recognition for facial recognition and object tracking.

Object Detection

Object detection is an extension of image recognition that not only identifies objects within an image but also locates and outlines their positions. It enables machines to understand not just what's in an image but where it is, making it a crucial tool in various AI applications.

Key Components of Object Detection

To understand object detection, let's break down its key components:

1. **Bounding Boxes:** Object detection models use bounding boxes to specify the location of objects within an image.
2. **CNNs with Additional Layers:** Object detection models build upon image recognition models by adding layers that predict bounding box coordinates and class probabilities.
3. **Training Data:** Similar to image recognition, object detection models require labeled datasets with images and bounding box annotations.
4. **Non-Maximum Suppression:** After detection, a post-processing step called non-maximum suppression is used to filter out redundant or overlapping bounding boxes.

How Object Detection Works

The operation of object detection can be summarized in several steps:

1. **Data Collection:** A dataset containing images and bounding box annotations is collected and prepared for training.
2. **Data Preprocessing:** Image data is preprocessed, and bounding box coordinates are normalized.
3. **Feature Extraction:** CNNs analyze images to extract features, while additional layers predict bounding box coordinates and class probabilities.
4. **Training:** The model is trained on the labeled dataset to learn how to locate and classify objects within images.

5. **Prediction:** When presented with a new image, the trained model detects and classifies objects while providing bounding box coordinates.

Applications of Object Detection

Object detection has a wide range of applications, including:

1. **Autonomous Vehicles:** Object detection is critical for autonomous vehicles to detect and respond to pedestrians, other vehicles, and obstacles.
2. **Retail:** Retailers use object detection for inventory management, theft prevention, and enhancing the shopping experience.
3. **Healthcare:** Object detection assists in the identification and tracking of anatomical structures and abnormalities in medical images.
4. **Surveillance:** Security systems use object detection to monitor and identify individuals, vehicles, and suspicious activities.
5. **Industrial Automation:** Object detection is employed in manufacturing for quality control and defect detection.

Challenges in Image Recognition and Object Detection

While image recognition and object detection have made significant strides, they face challenges such as:

1. **Scale and Resolution:** Handling images of different scales and resolutions can be challenging for models.
2. **Occlusion:** Objects partially or fully occluded in images can pose difficulties for detection.
3. **Variability:** Variations in lighting, viewpoint, and object appearance can impact recognition and detection accuracy.
4. **Training Data:** Annotated datasets must be extensive and diverse to train models effectively.
5. **Real-Time Processing:** Real-time object detection in video feeds requires high computational efficiency.

The Future of Image Recognition and Object Detection

The future holds promising developments in image recognition and object detection:

1. **Real-time Processing:** Advancements in hardware and algorithms will enable real-time object detection and recognition on a broader scale.

2. **Robustness:** Models will become more robust, capable of handling diverse conditions and environments.

3. **Multi-modal Integration:** Integration with other sensory data, such as audio and lidar, will enhance perception in autonomous systems.

4. **Customization:** More businesses will develop customized image recognition and object detection models for specific applications.

5. **AI Ethics:** Ethical considerations around privacy and bias in image recognition and object detection will become increasingly important.

Image recognition and object detection represent AI's visionary capabilities, enabling machines to understand and interact with the visual world. Image recognition categorizes and identifies objects within images, while object detection goes further, locating and outlining those objects. These technologies have transformative applications across industries, from healthcare and autonomous vehicles to retail and security.

As AI continues to advance, image recognition and object detection will play pivotal roles in shaping the future of technology and enhancing human-computer interaction. Understanding their fundamentals is essential for anyone interested in AI, computer vision, or the ever-evolving world of artificial intelligence.

Facial Recognition Technology: Unveiling the Future of Identity Verification

Facial recognition technology has emerged as a prominent and transformative facet of artificial intelligence (AI).

It brings the capability to identify and verify individuals based on their facial features, revolutionizing various aspects of our lives, from security and surveillance to authentication and personalization.

Facial Recognition Technology: A Brief Overview

Facial recognition technology, a subset of computer vision, involves the identification, verification, and categorization of individuals by analyzing and comparing their facial features. It harnesses the power of AI algorithms to recognize unique facial patterns, such as the arrangement of eyes, nose, and mouth, and employs these patterns to establish a person's identity.

Key Components of Facial Recognition Technology

To understand facial recognition technology, let's break down its key components:

1. **Face Detection:** The process begins with face detection, where AI algorithms locate and extract faces from images or video frames.
2. **Feature Extraction:** Facial landmarks and features, such as the distance between the eyes or the shape of the mouth, are extracted to create a facial template.
3. **Template Matching:** The extracted features are compared to a database of known faces or templates to establish a match.
4. **Machine Learning:** Supervised machine learning techniques are used to train the system to identify and verify individuals accurately.

5. **Liveness Detection:** To prevent spoofing or fraudulent attempts, systems often include liveness detection to ensure the face being scanned is a live, present face rather than a photograph or video.

How Facial Recognition Works

The operation of facial recognition technology can be summarized in several steps:

1. **Enrollment:** During enrollment, an individual's facial features are captured and converted into a unique template stored in a database.

2. **Face Detection:** When a person seeks verification or identification, the system detects and extracts their facial features from an image or video.

3. **Feature Extraction:** The system identifies facial landmarks and extracts features from the detected face.

4. **Template Comparison:** The extracted features are compared to the templates in the database to find a match.

5. **Verification or Identification:** Based on the comparison results, the system either verifies the identity of the individual (if they claim to be a specific person) or identifies them by retrieving their stored identity.

Applications of Facial Recognition Technology

Facial recognition technology has found diverse applications, including:

1. **Security and Surveillance:** It enhances security by identifying potential threats and monitoring public spaces for criminal activity.

2. **Access Control:** It provides secure access to buildings, devices, or data, reducing the reliance on traditional methods like passwords or cards.

3. **Payment Authentication:** Some payment systems use facial recognition for secure and convenient payment authorization.

4. **Personalization:** It enables personalized user experiences, such as tailored advertisements and content recommendations.

5. **Border Control and Immigration:** It expedites immigration processes by automating identity verification at borders.

6. **Law Enforcement:** Law enforcement agencies use it for criminal investigations and identifying missing persons.

Challenges and Concerns

Despite its transformative potential, facial recognition technology raises several challenges and concerns:

1. **Privacy:** The widespread deployment of facial recognition systems has sparked concerns about personal privacy and surveillance.

2. **Bias:** Biases in the algorithms can lead to misidentification, with certain demographic groups facing higher error rates.

3. **Accuracy:** The accuracy of facial recognition can vary based on factors such as image quality and lighting conditions.

4. **Security:** As with any technology, facial recognition systems can be vulnerable to hacking or spoofing.

5. **Consent:** There are ethical questions regarding obtaining consent from individuals before their facial data is collected and used.

The Future of Facial Recognition Technology

The future of facial recognition technology holds exciting developments and considerations:

1. **Improved Accuracy:** Ongoing research aims to enhance the accuracy of facial recognition, reducing errors and biases.

2. **Ethical Frameworks:** The industry is moving towards establishing ethical guidelines for the responsible use of facial recognition.

3. **Regulation:** Governments and regulatory bodies are considering legislation to address privacy concerns and establish guidelines for usage.

4. **Multimodal Biometrics:** Combining facial recognition with other biometric modalities, such as fingerprint or iris scans, will enhance security.

5. **AI Advancements:** Advances in AI and deep learning will continue to refine facial recognition capabilities.

Facial recognition technology represents a transformative force in AI, enabling machines to identify and verify individuals based on their unique facial features. Its applications span a wide spectrum, from enhancing security and access control to personalization and convenience. However, it also raises important ethical and privacy concerns that necessitate careful consideration and regulation.

As facial recognition technology continues to evolve, it has the potential to reshape various aspects of our lives. Understanding its fundamentals is essential for anyone interested in AI, biometrics, or the future of identity verification.

Robotics and Autonomous Systems

AI in Robotics: Transforming Automation and Beyond

Artificial Intelligence (AI) and robotics have forged a powerful synergy that is reshaping industries and redefining the boundaries of automation.

The integration of AI technologies into robotics has unleashed a new era of intelligent machines capable of adapting, learning, and performing complex tasks.

AI in Robotics: A Dynamic Partnership

AI and robotics have converged to create a dynamic partnership that empowers robots with cognitive capabilities, enabling them to operate in unpredictable environments, make decisions, and learn from experiences. This integration is at the heart of many cutting-edge applications, from autonomous vehicles and smart manufacturing to healthcare and space exploration.

Key Components of AI in Robotics

To understand AI in robotics, it is essential to grasp its key components:

1. **Sensors:** Robots are equipped with a variety of sensors, including cameras, lidar, radar, and tactile sensors, to perceive their surroundings.
2. **Machine Learning Algorithms:** AI-driven machine learning algorithms, such as neural networks, are employed to process sensor data, make decisions, and improve performance over time.
3. **Control Systems:** AI-powered control systems govern the robot's movements, ensuring precision and adaptability in dynamic environments.
4. **Autonomy:** AI allows robots to operate autonomously, without constant human intervention, by analyzing data and making real-time decisions.

How AI Enhances Robotics

The operation of AI in robotics can be summarized in several steps:

1. **Perception:** Sensors capture data about the robot's environment, including objects, obstacles, and terrain.
2. **Data Processing:** AI algorithms process the sensory data, extracting valuable information and identifying patterns.
3. **Decision-Making:** Based on the processed data, the robot's AI makes decisions regarding navigation, task execution, or problem-solving.
4. **Feedback Loop:** Robots continuously learn and adapt through a feedback loop, improving their performance with each interaction and experience.

Applications of AI in Robotics

The integration of AI in robotics has led to transformative applications across various industries, including:

1. **Autonomous Vehicles:** Self-driving cars and drones use AI to perceive and navigate through complex environments safely.
2. **Manufacturing:** Robots with AI capabilities enhance automation in manufacturing, enabling tasks such as quality control, pick-and-place, and assembly.
3. **Healthcare:** Surgical robots assist in minimally invasive surgeries, while AI-powered exoskeletons aid in rehabilitation.
4. **Space Exploration:** AI-driven rovers and spacecraft navigate and explore distant planets, making critical decisions in real-time.
5. **Agriculture:** Agricultural robots employ AI to perform tasks like crop monitoring, precision farming, and fruit picking.

Challenges and Considerations

While AI in robotics holds immense potential, it also presents challenges and considerations:

1. **Safety:** Ensuring the safety of AI-driven robots, especially in critical applications like healthcare and autonomous vehicles, remains a paramount concern.

2. **Ethical Dilemmas:** The use of AI in robotics raises ethical questions about decision-making in ambiguous situations and accountability for autonomous actions.

3. **Data Privacy:** AI robots often collect and process vast amounts of data, necessitating robust data privacy measures.

4. **Human-AI Interaction:** Designing intuitive interfaces for humans to interact with AI-driven robots is a challenge in user experience.

5. **Regulatory Frameworks:** Developing regulatory frameworks that govern AI and robotics is essential to address safety, ethical, and legal concerns.

The Future of AI in Robotics

The future of AI in robotics is brimming with potential:

1. **AI Advancements:** Ongoing advancements in AI, including reinforcement learning and natural language processing, will enhance the capabilities of robots.

2. **Human-Robot Collaboration:** Collaborative robots (cobots) will become more prevalent, working alongside humans in shared workspaces.

3. **Personal Robotics:** Personal robots capable of assisting with household tasks and providing companionship will become more sophisticated.

4. **Healthcare Robotics:** Robots will play a more significant role in healthcare, from diagnostics to patient care and even mental health support.

5. **Education and Research:** Educational and research robots will empower students and researchers to explore AI and robotics.

The integration of AI in robotics is at the forefront of technological innovation, revolutionizing industries and redefining automation. These intelligent machines, endowed with perception, decision-making, and learning capabilities, hold the promise of enhancing our lives in countless ways. However, they also pose complex challenges, from ensuring safety to navigating ethical and regulatory landscapes.

As AI continues to evolve and robots become more intelligent and adaptable, the possibilities are boundless. Understanding the dynamics of this ever-evolving partnership between AI and robotics is vital for anyone interested in the future of automation, technology, and human-machine interaction.

Self-Driving Cars and Drones: Transforming Transportation and Beyond

Self-driving cars and drones represent two remarkable innovations at the intersection of artificial intelligence (AI) and transportation technology.

These autonomous vehicles are revolutionizing how we move people and goods, offering safer, more efficient, and eco-friendly alternatives

Self-Driving Cars

Self-driving cars, also known as autonomous vehicles or driverless cars, are automobiles equipped with AI and sensor technology that can operate without human intervention. They have the potential to reshape the future of transportation by enhancing safety, reducing traffic congestion, and increasing accessibility.

Key Components of Self-Driving Cars

Understanding self-driving cars involves recognizing their key components:

1. **Sensors:** Self-driving cars are equipped with various sensors, including cameras, lidar, radar, and ultrasonic sensors, to perceive their surroundings.
2. **Control Systems:** AI-driven control systems process data from sensors and make real-time decisions, such as steering, accelerating, and braking.
3. **Mapping and Localization:** Self-driving cars rely on detailed maps and GPS data for precise navigation and location identification.
4. **Machine Learning:** Machine learning algorithms are used to train self-driving car systems to recognize and respond to various traffic situations.
5. **Connectivity:** These vehicles are often connected to the internet, enabling communication with other vehicles and infrastructure for enhanced safety and navigation.

How Self-Driving Cars Work

The operation of self-driving cars can be summarized in several steps:

1. **Perception:** Sensors capture data about the vehicle's environment, including other vehicles, pedestrians, road signs, and traffic signals.

2. **Data Processing:** AI algorithms process the sensor data, creating a real-time understanding of the vehicle's surroundings.

3. **Decision-Making:** The AI control system uses the processed data to make driving decisions, such as changing lanes, stopping at intersections, or avoiding obstacles.

4. **Navigation:** Self-driving cars use mapping and GPS data to plan routes and stay on course.

5. **Feedback Loop:** Machine learning models continuously improve the vehicle's performance and decision-making through feedback from real-world driving experiences.

Applications of Self-Driving Cars

The adoption of self-driving cars has far-reaching implications, with applications including:

1. **Ride-Sharing Services:** Companies like Uber and Lyft are investing in autonomous vehicles to offer driverless ride-sharing services.

2. **Cargo Transportation:** Autonomous trucks and delivery vehicles promise to revolutionize logistics and supply chain management.

3. **Accessibility:** Self-driving cars have the potential to provide mobility solutions for the elderly and disabled, offering increased independence.

4. **Urban Planning:** Cities may be redesigned with fewer parking spaces and more green areas, as self-driving cars reduce the need for parking.

5. **Traffic Management:** Autonomous vehicles can communicate with each other to optimize traffic flow and reduce congestion.

Challenges and Considerations

While self-driving cars hold significant promise, they also present challenges and considerations:

1. **Safety:** Ensuring the safety of autonomous vehicles, including protection against cyberattacks, is paramount.
2. **Regulation:** Developing comprehensive regulations and standards for self-driving cars is essential to ensure consistency and safety.
3. **Ethical Dilemmas:** AI algorithms must be programmed to make ethical decisions in situations where choices may involve potential harm.
4. **Transition Period:** Transitioning from traditional vehicles to self-driving cars poses infrastructure and compatibility challenges.
5. **Job Displacement:** The rise of autonomous vehicles may lead to job displacement for professional drivers.

The Future of Self-Driving Cars

The future of self-driving cars is brimming with possibilities:

1. **Level 5 Autonomy:** Achieving level 5 autonomy, where vehicles require no human intervention, remains a long-term goal.
2. **Improved Safety:** As AI and sensor technologies advance, self-driving cars are likely to become safer than human-driven vehicles.
3. **Environmental Impact:** Reduced traffic congestion and more efficient driving could lead to a decrease in greenhouse gas emissions.
4. **Mobility-as-a-Service (MaaS):** The concept of MaaS, where transportation is viewed as a service rather than ownership, could become more prevalent with self-driving cars.
5. **Smart Cities:** Self-driving cars will play a central role in the development of smart cities, optimizing transportation and urban planning.

Drones

Drones, also known as unmanned aerial vehicles (UAVs), are autonomous or remotely operated aircraft that have gained prominence in a wide range of industries and applications. They are equipped with AI-driven technologies that enable them to perform tasks such as aerial photography, surveillance, delivery, and more.

Key Components of Drones

Understanding drones involves recognizing their key components:

1. **Sensors:** Drones are equipped with various sensors, including cameras, lidar, and GPS, to navigate and collect data.

2. **Control Systems:** AI algorithms govern the flight, navigation, and data processing capabilities of drones.

3. **Communication:** Drones often rely on wireless communication to transmit data to remote operators or central control centers.

4. **Battery Technology:** Advances in battery technology have extended the flight time and range of drones.

How Drones Work

The operation of drones can be summarized in several steps:

1. **Takeoff:** Drones take off and ascend to the desired altitude, guided by GPS and onboard sensors.

2. **Data Collection:** Drones use sensors to collect data or capture images and videos of the target area.

3. **Data Processing:** AI algorithms process the collected data to extract meaningful information or detect anomalies.

4. **Navigation:** Drones can navigate autonomously using GPS waypoints or respond to real-time commands from operators.

5. **Mission Execution:** Drones carry out specific missions, such as aerial surveys, package delivery, or search and rescue operations.

Applications of Drones

Drones have found applications across various domains, including:

1. **Agriculture:** Drones assist in crop monitoring, pest control, and precision agriculture.
2. **Infrastructure Inspection:** They are used for inspecting bridges, power lines, and pipelines, reducing the need for human inspectors in hazardous environments.
3. **Disaster Response:** Drones aid in search and rescue operations, delivering supplies to disaster-stricken areas, and assessing damage.
4. **Film and Photography:** Drones provide unique aerial perspectives for filmmaking, photography, and sports coverage.
5. **Environmental Monitoring:** They are deployed for wildlife tracking, habitat assessment, and environmental research.

Challenges and Considerations

Despite their versatility, drones also pose challenges and considerations:

1. **Regulation:** Developing regulations for drone operations, including issues related to airspace and privacy, is a complex task.
2. **Safety:** Ensuring safe drone operations, especially in crowded airspace, is a critical concern.
3. **Security:** Protecting drones from hacking or misuse is essential, especially in sensitive applications like surveillance and delivery.
4. **Battery Life:** Extending drone battery life remains a challenge, limiting the duration and range of missions.

5. **Public Perception:** Addressing concerns about privacy and noise pollution is crucial for broader drone acceptance.

The Future of Drones

The future of drones is filled with innovation and potential:

1. **Advanced Sensors:** Drones will benefit from advancements in sensor technologies, enabling more sophisticated data collection and analysis.
2. **AI Autonomy:** Enhanced AI algorithms will empower drones to make real-time decisions and adapt to changing conditions.
3. **Delivery Services:** Drone delivery services may become more commonplace, revolutionizing e-commerce and logistics.
4. **Urban Air Mobility (UAM):** UAM concepts envision air taxis and personal flying vehicles powered by drone technology.
5. **Environmental Monitoring:** Drones will play a vital role in monitoring climate change, wildlife conservation, and disaster prediction.

Self-driving cars and drones represent the forefront of AI-driven transportation technology, promising safer, more efficient, and environmentally friendly modes of travel and service. While both face challenges related to safety, regulation, and ethics, they hold immense potential to transform industries and improve our lives.

Understanding the dynamics of self-driving cars and drones is essential for anyone interested in the future of transportation, technology, and autonomous systems. These innovations are poised to reshape how we move people and goods and explore new frontiers of possibility.

Ethics and AI

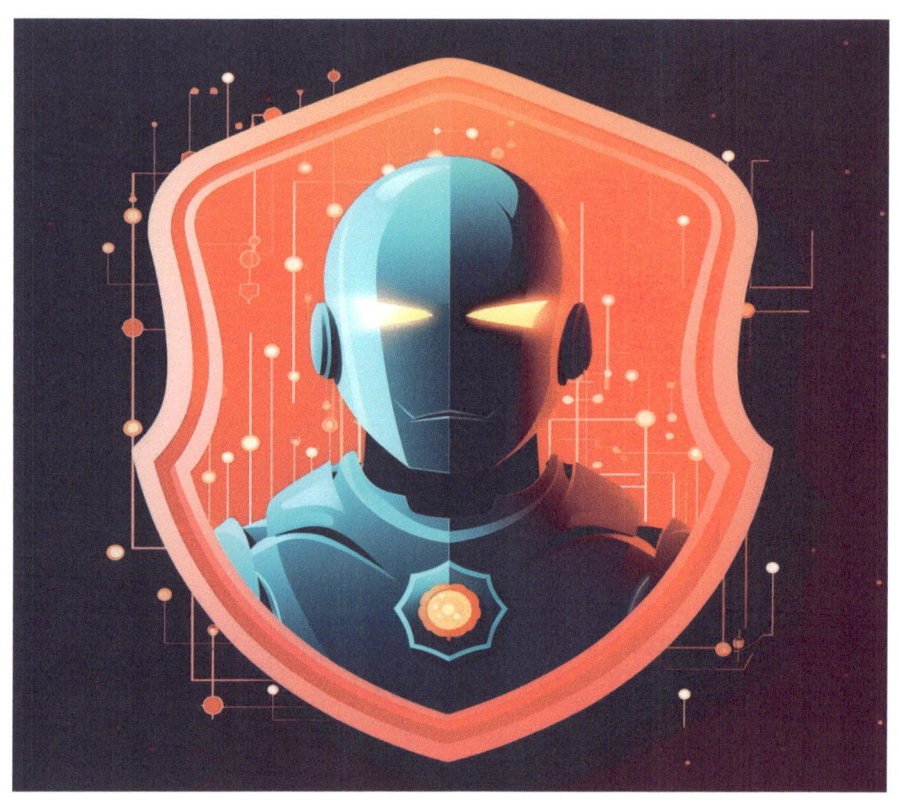

Addressing Bias and Ensuring Fairness in AI Systems

Artificial Intelligence (AI) has made remarkable strides in recent years, transforming various aspects of our lives, from healthcare and finance to education and transportation.

However, the rapid proliferation of AI technologies has also brought to light a pressing concern: the ethical implications of AI systems, particularly issues related to bias and fairness.

Ethics in AI

Ethics in AI refers to the moral principles and values that guide the development, deployment, and use of artificial intelligence systems. The ethical considerations surrounding AI are critical, as these systems have the potential to affect individuals, communities, and societies on a global scale. Key ethical principles in AI include transparency, accountability, privacy, and fairness.

Bias in AI

Bias in AI refers to the presence of systematic and unfair discrimination in the outcomes or decisions produced by AI systems. This bias can occur when AI algorithms are trained on biased data or when the design and implementation of AI systems inadvertently reinforce existing prejudices. Bias in AI can manifest in various forms, including racial, gender, and socioeconomic bias.

Key Components of Bias in AI

Understanding bias in AI involves recognizing its key components:

1. **Training Data Bias:** If the training data used to teach AI algorithms contains biases, the AI system is likely to replicate and amplify those biases in its decision-making processes.

2. **Algorithmic Bias:** Some AI algorithms themselves may be inherently biased due to their design or the data they are trained on, leading to unfair outcomes.

3. **Human Bias:** Human programmers and data annotators can introduce their biases consciously or unconsciously during the development of AI systems.

4. **Feedback Loop:** AI systems can perpetuate bias through a feedback loop, as they make decisions based on historical data, which may contain biased outcomes.

Impact of Bias in AI

The impact of bias in AI can be profound and wide-ranging:

1. **Discrimination:** Biased AI systems can perpetuate discrimination against certain groups, reinforcing existing inequalities.

2. **Unfair Treatment:** Bias can lead to unfair treatment in various domains, including lending, hiring, and criminal justice.

3. **Lack of Trust:** Biased AI erodes trust in the technology and its developers, hindering its adoption and acceptance.

4. **Reputation Damage:** Companies and organizations that deploy biased AI systems may face reputational damage and legal consequences.

Addressing Bias and Ensuring Fairness in AI Systems

To mitigate bias and ensure fairness in AI systems, several strategies and best practices are employed:

1. **Diverse and Representative Data:** AI developers must ensure that the training data used is diverse and representative of the populations the AI system will interact with.

2. **Bias Auditing:** Regular audits and assessments of AI systems for bias are essential to identify and rectify potential issues.

3. **Algorithmic Fairness:** Researchers are developing algorithms that prioritize fairness and minimize bias in AI decision-making.

4. **Ethical Guidelines:** Companies and organizations should adhere to ethical guidelines and codes of conduct when designing and deploying AI systems.

5. **Human Oversight:** Human intervention and oversight are critical to ensuring that AI systems make ethical and unbiased decisions.

6. **Diversity in Development:** Encouraging diversity in AI development teams can help reduce the likelihood of biased AI systems.

The Role of Regulation

The role of government and regulatory bodies is crucial in addressing bias and ensuring fairness in AI systems. Some key initiatives include:

1. **Data Privacy Laws:** Regulations like the General Data Protection Regulation (GDPR) in Europe emphasize the importance of data protection and individual rights in AI systems.

2. **Algorithmic Transparency:** Governments are exploring regulations that require companies to disclose how AI algorithms make decisions.

3. **Anti-Discrimination Laws:** Existing anti-discrimination laws may need to be updated to address bias in AI decision-making.

4. **Ethical AI Certification:** Some proposals advocate for certification processes that assess the ethical and fairness aspects of AI systems before deployment.

Challenges in Ensuring Fairness

Despite ongoing efforts, ensuring fairness in AI systems remains a complex challenge:

1. **Data Availability:** Obtaining unbiased, diverse, and representative data can be difficult, especially in cases where historical data contains inherent biases.

2. **Algorithm Complexity:** Many AI algorithms are complex and may exhibit biased behavior that is challenging to detect and correct.

3. **Trade-offs:** Balancing fairness with other objectives, such as accuracy or efficiency, can be a delicate trade-off.

4. **Bias Mitigation:** Bias mitigation techniques may inadvertently introduce new biases or reduce the system's overall performance.

5. **Emergent Bias:** Bias can emerge in AI systems even when the initial training data is unbiased, making it challenging to predict and prevent.

The Future of Ethical AI

The future of ethical AI hinges on ongoing research, technological advancements, and collective efforts to address bias and ensure fairness. Key developments include:

1. **Fairness-Aware AI:** Researchers are actively working on fairness-aware AI models that prioritize ethical decision-making.

2. **Explainability and Interpretability:** AI systems are being designed to provide explanations for their decisions, allowing users to understand their behavior better.

3. **Bias Detection Tools:** The development of automated bias detection tools will aid in identifying and rectifying bias in AI systems.

4. **Ethical AI Frameworks:** The establishment of ethical AI frameworks and guidelines will shape the responsible development and deployment of AI.

Ethics and fairness in AI are paramount considerations as AI technologies continue to advance and permeate various aspects of our lives. Bias in AI systems can have far-reaching consequences, from perpetuating discrimination to eroding trust in technology. Addressing bias and ensuring fairness in AI is a collective responsibility, involving developers, researchers, governments, and society at large. By adhering to ethical principles, embracing diversity, and employing technological advancements, we can pave the way for a future where AI systems are both powerful and just, contributing positively to our world.

Privacy and Security Concerns in the Age of Technology

As we continue to witness rapid advancements in technology, our lives have become increasingly intertwined with the digital world.

While these technological innovations have brought numerous conveniences and benefits, they have also given rise to significant privacy and security concerns.

Privacy Concerns

Privacy concerns in the digital age revolve around the protection of personal information, the right to control one's data, and the potential for surveillance and data misuse. Key privacy concerns include:

1. **Data Collection:** Companies and organizations collect vast amounts of personal data, including browsing habits, location data, and social media interactions, often without explicit consent.

2. **Data Breaches:** High-profile data breaches expose sensitive information, such as credit card numbers and personal identifiers, leaving individuals vulnerable to identity theft and fraud.

3. **Surveillance:** Mass surveillance programs by governments and corporations have raised concerns about the erosion of individual privacy rights.

4. **Profiling:** The use of algorithms to create detailed user profiles for targeted advertising can lead to invasions of privacy and manipulation of user behavior.

5. **Lack of Consent:** Individuals may not be fully aware of the data they are sharing or how it will be used, leading to concerns about informed consent.

Security Concerns

Security concerns encompass threats to the confidentiality, integrity, and availability of data and systems. Key security concerns include:

1. **Cyberattacks:** The rise of cyberattacks, including ransomware, malware, and phishing, poses a significant threat to individuals and organizations.

2. **Data Loss:** Inadequate data backup and recovery mechanisms can result in data loss due to hardware failure, human error, or cyberattacks.

3. **IoT Vulnerabilities:** The proliferation of Internet of Things (IoT) devices has introduced new security vulnerabilities, as many of these devices lack robust security features.

4. **Social Engineering:** Attackers often exploit human psychology through social engineering tactics to gain unauthorized access to systems and data.

5. **Weak Passwords:** The use of weak or easily guessable passwords remains a common security issue, allowing attackers to gain unauthorized access to accounts.

Privacy and Security in the Digital Age

In the digital age, privacy and security concerns are intertwined, as individuals' personal data becomes a prime target for malicious actors. Ensuring both privacy and security requires a multifaceted approach:

1. **Data Encryption:** Encrypting data both in transit and at rest can safeguard it from unauthorized access, even in the event of a breach.

2. **Two-Factor Authentication (2FA):** Implementing 2FA adds an extra layer of security to accounts, making them less vulnerable to unauthorized access.

3. **Regular Updates:** Keeping software, operating systems, and devices up to date is crucial to patch known security vulnerabilities.

4. **Security Awareness:** Promoting security awareness among users can help prevent falling victim to social engineering attacks.

5. **Privacy Settings:** Reviewing and adjusting privacy settings on devices and online services can limit the amount of personal data that is collected and shared.

Emerging Technologies and Privacy

The advent of emerging technologies like artificial intelligence (AI), biometrics, and blockchain introduces new privacy and security considerations:

1. **AI and Privacy:** AI algorithms can process vast amounts of data to draw insights and make predictions, but concerns about bias, transparency, and data privacy arise in the process.

2. **Biometrics and Security:** Biometric authentication, such as fingerprint and facial recognition, offers convenience but also raises concerns about data protection and security.

3. **Blockchain and Data Security:** Blockchain technology has the potential to enhance data security and privacy by providing immutable and transparent records.

Government Regulation and Privacy Laws

Governments around the world are enacting privacy laws and regulations to address the growing concerns about data privacy. Key regulations include:

1. **General Data Protection Regulation (GDPR):** The GDPR in Europe imposes strict rules on data protection, requiring organizations to obtain informed consent and notify individuals of data breaches.

2. **California Consumer Privacy Act (CCPA):** The CCPA grants California residents certain rights over their personal data and requires businesses to provide transparency about data practices.

3. **Health Insurance Portability and Accountability Act (HIPAA):** HIPAA in the United States safeguards the privacy and security of health information.

4. **Children's Online Privacy Protection Act (COPPA):** COPPA imposes regulations on online services that collect data from children under 13 years old.

Challenges and Considerations

Despite regulatory efforts, challenges in addressing privacy and security concerns persist:

1. **Global Nature of Data:** Data flows across borders, making it challenging to enforce regulations and maintain consistent privacy standards worldwide.

2. **Balancing Security and Privacy:** Striking a balance between robust security measures and protecting user privacy can be a complex endeavor.

3. **Evolving Threat Landscape:** Cyberthreats are continually evolving, requiring organizations to adapt and enhance their security measures.

4. **Ethical Considerations:** Ethical concerns about data usage, including issues of consent and transparency, continue to evolve.

5. **User Education:** Ensuring that individuals are informed about privacy and security practices remains a significant challenge.

The Future of Privacy and Security

The future of privacy and security will be shaped by ongoing technological developments, regulatory changes, and societal attitudes. Key trends include:

1. **Privacy by Design:** Implementing privacy and security measures from the inception of technologies and systems.

2. **AI-Driven Security:** Leveraging AI to detect and respond to security threats in real-time.

3. **User-Controlled Data:** Empowering individuals with greater control over their data and how it is used.

4. **Global Privacy Frameworks:** The development of global frameworks for data privacy and security.

5. **Ethical Considerations:** Heightened awareness of the ethical implications of data collection and use.

Privacy and security concerns in the digital age are paramount, as our reliance on technology continues to grow. Addressing these concerns requires a collective effort from individuals, organizations, governments, and technology developers. Striking the right balance between privacy and security while adapting to evolving threats and regulatory changes will be essential in ensuring a safer and more privacy-respecting digital future.

Real-World Applications of AI

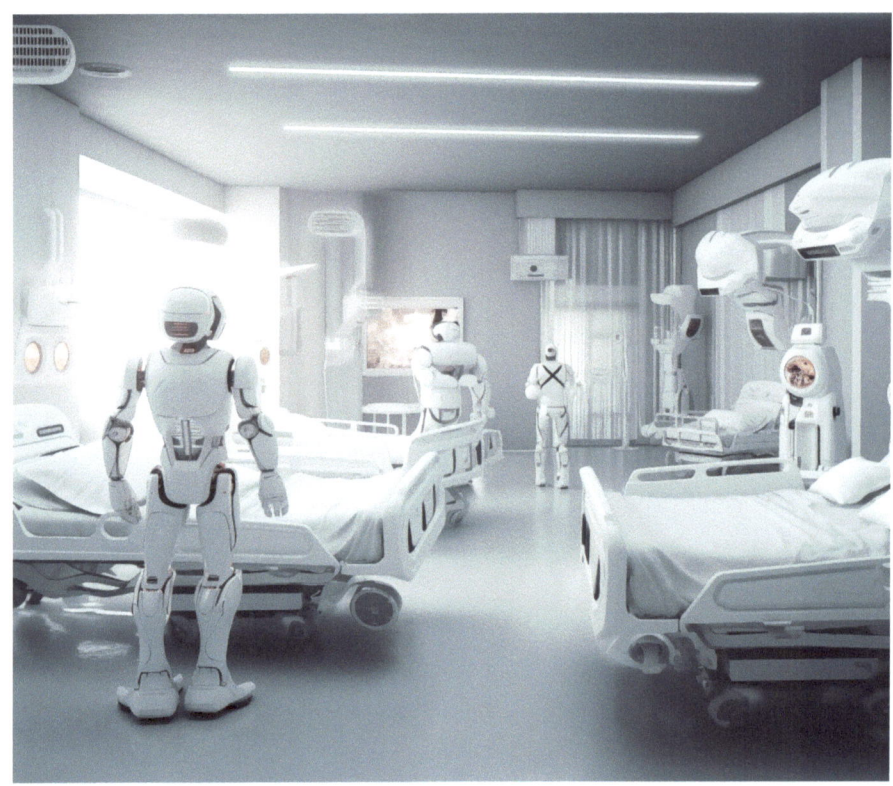

Transforming Healthcare, Finance, and Retail

Artificial Intelligence (AI) has evolved from a futuristic concept to a transformative force in various industries, reshaping the way businesses operate and deliver services.

AI in Healthcare

AI has made substantial inroads into healthcare, promising improved patient care, enhanced diagnostics, and streamlined administrative processes.

1. **Disease Diagnosis and Prediction:** AI-powered algorithms can analyze medical data, such as images, patient records, and genetic information, to assist in the diagnosis and prediction of diseases like cancer, diabetes, and heart conditions. For instance, IBM's Watson for Oncology uses AI to analyze patient data and recommend personalized cancer treatment options.

2. **Radiology and Imaging:** AI-driven image analysis has revolutionized radiology by improving the accuracy and speed of diagnosing conditions like fractures, tumors, and neurological disorders. Companies like Aidoc employ deep learning to assist radiologists in detecting abnormalities in medical images.

3. **Drug Discovery:** AI accelerates drug discovery processes by analyzing vast datasets to identify potential drug candidates, predict their effectiveness, and simulate their interactions with biological systems. Insilico Medicine, for example, employs AI to discover novel molecules for drug development.

4. **Personalized Medicine:** AI facilitates the development of personalized treatment plans based on an individual's genetic makeup and medical history. This approach ensures more effective and targeted therapies, minimizing adverse effects.

5. **Healthcare Chatbots:** AI-powered chatbots provide 24/7 support for patients, answering questions, scheduling appointments, and even monitoring chronic conditions. Ada Health's AI chatbot helps users assess symptoms and seek appropriate medical advice.

AI in Finance

The finance industry has harnessed AI to improve risk assessment, fraud detection, and customer service while optimizing investment strategies.

1. **Algorithmic Trading:** AI-driven algorithms analyze vast amounts of financial data to execute high-frequency trades and optimize investment portfolios. These algorithms adapt to market conditions and execute trades with precision and speed.

2. **Fraud Detection:** AI models employ machine learning to detect fraudulent activities in real-time by analyzing transaction patterns, user behavior, and historical data. This safeguards financial institutions and their customers from cybercrime.

3. **Credit Scoring:** AI-powered credit scoring models evaluate creditworthiness more accurately by considering a broader range of data, including social media activity and transaction history. This enables lenders to make more informed lending decisions.

4. **Customer Service:** Chatbots and virtual assistants powered by AI enhance customer service by addressing inquiries, resolving issues, and providing personalized recommendations. They offer efficient and responsive support, improving customer satisfaction.

5. **Robo-Advisors:** AI-driven robo-advisors offer automated, low-cost investment advice and portfolio management, making investing accessible to a broader audience. Companies like Wealthfront and Betterment leverage AI to provide tailored investment strategies.

AI in Retail

The retail industry has embraced AI to enhance customer experiences, optimize supply chains, and drive sales.

1. **Recommendation Engines:** AI-driven recommendation systems, such as those used by Amazon and Netflix, analyze user behavior and preferences to offer personalized product recommendations. This boosts customer engagement and sales.

2. **Inventory Management:** AI-powered demand forecasting and inventory optimization algorithms help retailers minimize stockouts, reduce excess inventory, and optimize supply chains. This results in cost savings and improved customer satisfaction.

3. **Visual Search and Image Recognition:** AI enables customers to search for products using images, making it easier to find desired items. Pinterest's Lens and Google Lens are examples of AI-driven visual search tools.

4. **Pricing Optimization:** Retailers use AI to dynamically adjust pricing based on factors like demand, competition, and historical sales data. This maximizes profitability and ensures competitive pricing.

5. **Chatbots and Virtual Assistants:** AI chatbots assist customers with inquiries, orders, and returns, offering a seamless shopping experience and reducing the workload on customer service teams.

Challenges and Considerations

While AI brings significant benefits to healthcare, finance, and retail, it also presents challenges and considerations:

1. **Data Privacy:** Handling sensitive customer data requires robust data privacy measures and compliance with regulations like GDPR.

2. **Ethical Concerns:** Ensuring ethical use of AI, particularly in healthcare, where decisions impact lives, is crucial. Transparency and accountability are essential.

3. **Data Quality:** AI models heavily depend on the quality of data. Inaccurate or biased data can lead to flawed predictions and decisions.

4. **Regulatory Compliance:** Staying abreast of evolving regulations and ensuring compliance is a continuous challenge, especially in finance and healthcare.

5. **Integration:** Integrating AI solutions seamlessly into existing workflows and systems can be complex and costly.

The Future of AI in These Sectors

The future of AI in healthcare, finance, and retail is characterized by ongoing innovation and expansion:

1. **Healthcare:** AI is expected to play an increasingly significant role in early disease detection, drug discovery, and remote patient monitoring. Telehealth and AI-driven diagnostics are likely to become more commonplace.

2. **Finance:** AI will continue to evolve, enabling more sophisticated trading algorithms, personalized financial advice, and improved fraud detection. Central bank digital currencies (CBDCs) may leverage AI for security and transaction monitoring.

3. **Retail:** AI will offer more immersive and personalized shopping experiences through augmented reality (AR), virtual reality (VR), and AI-driven virtual storefronts. Sustainability and ethical sourcing will also be facilitated by AI-driven supply chain monitoring.

AI is reshaping healthcare, finance, and retail in profound ways, offering improved diagnostics, optimized financial strategies, and personalized shopping experiences. Despite challenges related to data privacy, ethics, and compliance, AI's transformative potential in these sectors is undeniable.

As technology continues to advance, the future holds even greater promise, with AI poised to revolutionize how we approach healthcare, financial services, and retail in the digital age.

The Future of AI in Different Sectors

Artificial Intelligence (AI) is poised to play an increasingly pivotal role in various sectors, revolutionizing the way businesses operate and services are delivered.

1. **Healthcare:** AI's future in healthcare is promising. We can expect AI-driven advancements in early disease detection, drug discovery, and personalized treatment plans. Machine learning algorithms will analyze vast patient datasets to identify subtle patterns and predict health outcomes.

   Telehealth and remote patient monitoring will become more sophisticated, providing access to healthcare services from anywhere. AI-powered robotic surgery and diagnostics will enhance precision and reduce errors.

2. **Finance:** In the financial sector, AI will continue to evolve, offering more accurate risk assessment, fraud detection, and personalized financial advice. Trading algorithms will become even more sophisticated, adapting to market conditions in real-time.

   Central banks may utilize AI for the management of digital currencies, enhancing security and transaction monitoring. AI-driven chatbots and virtual financial advisors will provide customers with personalized, 24/7 support.

3. **Retail:** AI's future in retail will focus on immersive and personalized shopping experiences. Augmented reality (AR) and virtual reality (VR) technologies will enable customers to interact with products in a virtual space. AI-driven recommendation systems will become more accurate, boosting customer engagement and sales.

   Sustainability and ethical sourcing will be facilitated by AI-driven supply chain monitoring, ensuring transparent and responsible practices.

4. **Education:** AI will transform education by providing personalized learning experiences. Adaptive learning platforms will cater to individual student needs, helping them grasp concepts at their own pace. AI tutors and virtual teachers will offer additional support to students, answering questions and providing explanations. Administrative tasks such as grading and scheduling will be automated, allowing educators to focus on teaching.

5. **Manufacturing:** AI's future in manufacturing lies in automation and predictive maintenance. AI-driven robots and autonomous systems will optimize production lines, reducing costs and improving efficiency. Predictive maintenance models will help prevent equipment breakdowns, minimizing downtime. AI will enhance quality control by identifying defects in real-time, ensuring consistent product quality.

6. **Transportation:** In the transportation sector, AI will lead to safer and more efficient travel. Self-driving cars and trucks will become more prevalent, reducing accidents and traffic congestion. AI-driven traffic management systems will optimize traffic flow in real-time. Drones and autonomous delivery vehicles will revolutionize logistics and last-mile delivery.

7. **Energy:** AI will contribute to sustainable energy solutions. Smart grids will use AI to balance energy supply and demand efficiently. Predictive maintenance will improve the reliability of renewable energy infrastructure. AI-driven energy management systems will help consumers reduce their carbon footprint by optimizing energy usage.

In conclusion, the future of AI is characterized by innovation and transformation across various sectors.

Whether it's improving healthcare outcomes, enhancing financial services, revolutionizing retail experiences, or transforming education, AI's potential is boundless.

Emerging Trends in AI

Quantum Computing and AI

Quantum Computing: A Brief Overview

Quantum computing represents a significant leap forward in the world of computing. Unlike classical computers that use bits to represent information as 0s and 1s, quantum computers use quantum bits or qubits.

Qubits can exist in multiple states simultaneously, thanks to the principles of superposition and entanglement. This unique property enables quantum computers to perform certain calculations exponentially faster than classical computers.

The Promise of Quantum Computing for AI

Quantum computing holds immense promise for the field of AI, with several emerging trends and potential applications:

1. **Optimization Problems:** Quantum computers excel at solving complex optimization problems. AI algorithms can leverage quantum computing to optimize logistics, supply chains, and financial portfolios with unprecedented speed and accuracy.

2. **Machine Learning Acceleration:** Quantum computing can enhance machine learning algorithms, reducing the time required to train deep neural networks. This can lead to breakthroughs in natural language processing, image recognition, and other AI applications.

3. **Drug Discovery:** AI-driven drug discovery relies on vast simulations and computations. Quantum computing can significantly accelerate the discovery of new pharmaceuticals by simulating complex molecular interactions more efficiently.

4. **Cryptography:** Quantum computing's potential to crack current encryption methods poses security challenges. However, it can also lead to the development of quantum-safe encryption techniques to protect AI systems and data.

Challenges and Considerations

While the fusion of quantum computing and AI is full of promise, it also presents challenges:

1. **Hardware Development:** Building practical and scalable quantum hardware remains a significant challenge. Quantum computers are highly sensitive to external factors and require extreme cooling conditions to operate effectively.

2. **Algorithm Development:** Adapting existing AI algorithms to quantum computing and developing new quantum machine learning algorithms require interdisciplinary collaboration and research.

3. **Cost:** Quantum computers are currently expensive to develop and maintain, limiting their accessibility to a select few organizations.

4. **Quantum Error Correction:** Overcoming the inherent error rates of quantum computers is essential for reliable and accurate AI applications.

The Future of Quantum Computing and AI

The future of quantum computing and AI is undoubtedly intertwined:

1. **Quantum Machine Learning:** Quantum machine learning algorithms will continue to evolve, offering practical advantages in solving real-world problems.

2. **Hybrid Approaches:** Hybrid quantum-classical AI models will become more prevalent, harnessing the strengths of both quantum and classical computing.

3. **Quantum Cloud Services:** As quantum computing becomes more accessible, cloud-based quantum services will emerge, allowing organizations to harness quantum power without owning quantum hardware.

4. **AI Ethics and Security:** As quantum computing advances, AI ethics and security will become even more critical. Ensuring the ethical use of AI and protecting AI systems from quantum threats will be paramount.

The convergence of quantum computing and AI represents one of the most exciting frontiers in technology. It holds the potential to transform industries, solve previously insurmountable problems, and revolutionize the field of artificial intelligence.

AI and the Internet of Things (IoT): A Transformative Partnership

As both an AI engineer and an English language professor, I am delighted to delve into the fascinating realm of AI's integration with the Internet of Things (IoT).

Understanding the Internet of Things (IoT)

The Internet of Things refers to a vast network of interconnected physical objects or "things" that are embedded with sensors, software, and connectivity, allowing them to collect and exchange data. These objects can range from everyday devices like thermostats and refrigerators to industrial machinery and vehicles. The IoT ecosystem has rapidly expanded, creating a wealth of data that can be harnessed for various purposes.

The Role of AI in the IoT

Artificial Intelligence plays a pivotal role in the IoT landscape, enhancing its capabilities in several ways:

1. **Data Processing and Analysis:** The sheer volume of data generated by IoT devices is overwhelming. AI algorithms can sift through this data, identifying patterns, anomalies, and insights that would be impossible for humans to discern.

2. **Predictive Maintenance:** AI can predict when IoT-connected machinery or devices are likely to fail, enabling proactive maintenance to prevent costly breakdowns and downtime.

3. **Automation and Optimization:** AI-driven automation can optimize processes and operations based on real-time data from IoT sensors. This can lead to energy savings, improved resource allocation, and increased efficiency

4. **Personalization:** AI can use data from IoT devices to deliver personalized experiences. For example, smart home devices can learn a user's preferences and adjust settings accordingly.

5. **Enhanced Security:** AI can bolster the security of IoT networks by identifying and mitigating cybersecurity threats in real-time.

Applications of AI and IoT

The integration of AI and IoT has far-reaching applications across various sectors:

1. **Smart Cities:** AI-enabled IoT sensors monitor traffic flow, reduce energy consumption, and improve public safety. For instance, smart traffic lights can optimize traffic patterns based on real-time data.

2. **Healthcare:** IoT devices equipped with AI can remotely monitor patients' health, predict disease outbreaks, and assist in the early diagnosis of medical conditions.

3. **Manufacturing:** AI-driven IoT solutions optimize production processes, improve product quality, and reduce waste by monitoring and adjusting manufacturing parameters.

4. **Agriculture:** IoT sensors combined with AI provide farmers with valuable insights into crop health, soil conditions, and irrigation management.

5. **Retail:** AI-powered analytics of IoT-generated data help retailers optimize inventory, improve the customer experience, and increase sales through personalized recommendations.

Challenges and Considerations

While the partnership between AI and IoT holds tremendous promise, it also presents challenges:

1. **Data Privacy:** The collection of vast amounts of data raises concerns about privacy and security. Protecting user data and ensuring compliance with regulations is paramount.

2. **Interoperability:** Ensuring that diverse IoT devices and AI systems can work together seamlessly is a complex challenge.

3. **Scalability:** As the number of IoT devices grows, ensuring that AI systems can handle the increasing data flow becomes critical.

The Future of AI and IoT

The future of AI and IoT is intertwined, with continued growth and innovation on the horizon:

1. **Edge AI:** AI algorithms will increasingly be deployed directly on IoT devices, reducing latency and enhancing real-time decision-making.

2. **5G Connectivity:** The rollout of 5G networks will provide the high-speed, low-latency connections required for AI-powered IoT applications to flourish.

3. **AI at Scale:** AI will continue to scale across industries, offering increasingly sophisticated solutions for IoT data analysis and decision-making.

The marriage of AI and IoT is transforming our world, enabling greater efficiency, personalization, and insight across a myriad of sectors.

Career Paths in AI

Roles in AI and Required Skills

Artificial Intelligence (AI) is a rapidly evolving field with a diverse range of roles and responsibilities.

1. Machine Learning Engineer

Machine Learning Engineers are responsible for designing, implementing, and maintaining machine learning models and systems.

Their primary tasks include data preprocessing, model development, and optimization.

Required Skills:
- Proficiency in programming languages such as Python or R.
- Strong understanding of machine learning algorithms and frameworks (e.g., TensorFlow, PyTorch).
- Data preprocessing skills, including data cleaning and feature engineering.
- Knowledge of deep learning and neural networks.
- Experience with model evaluation and hyperparameter tuning.

2. Data Scientist

Data Scientists analyze large datasets to extract valuable insights and make data-driven decisions. They work on various tasks, including data exploration, statistical analysis, and predictive modeling.

Required Skills:
- Strong programming skills in Python or R.
- Proficiency in data manipulation libraries like Pandas.
- Statistical analysis and hypothesis testing expertise.
- Data visualization using tools like Matplotlib or Seaborn.
- Machine learning knowledge for predictive modeling.

3. AI Research Scientist

AI Research Scientists focus on pushing the boundaries of AI technology through theoretical research and experimentation. They often work in academia or research labs.

Required Skills:

- A Ph.D. in a relevant field (computer science, machine learning, etc.).
- Strong analytical and problem-solving abilities.
- Proficiency in programming and deep understanding of AI theory.
- Research publication track record.
- Ability to design and conduct experiments.

4. AI Ethicist

AI Ethicists ensure that AI systems are developed and used responsibly and ethically. They address issues related to bias, fairness, transparency, and privacy in AI applications.

Required Skills:

- An understanding of ethical principles and their application in AI.
- Strong communication skills to engage with technical and non-technical stakeholders.
- Knowledge of AI bias mitigation techniques.
- Familiarity with AI regulations and guidelines.

5. AI Product Manager

AI Product Managers bridge the gap between technical development and business objectives. They define product goals, prioritize features, and oversee the development process.

Required Skills:

- Strong project management skills.

- An understanding of AI technology and its applications.
- Ability to translate business needs into technical requirements.
- Effective communication and leadership skills.

6. Natural Language Processing (NLP) Engineer

NLP Engineers specialize in developing AI systems that understand and generate human language. They work on tasks like sentiment analysis, language translation, and chatbot development.

Required Skills:
- Proficiency in programming languages like Python and knowledge of NLP libraries (NLTK, spaCy).
- Understanding of linguistic concepts and language models.
- Experience with deep learning models for NLP (BERT, GPT).
- Data preprocessing and text analysis skills.

7. Computer Vision Engineer

Computer Vision Engineers focus on developing AI systems that interpret and understand visual information from images and videos. They work on tasks like image recognition, object detection, and facial recognition.

Required Skills:
- Proficiency in programming languages like Python and knowledge of computer vision libraries (OpenCV, TensorFlow).
- Understanding of image processing techniques.
- Deep learning knowledge for building convolutional neural networks (CNNs).
- Experience with object detection and image classification.

8. AI DevOps Engineer

AI DevOps Engineers are responsible for deploying and maintaining AI models and systems in production environments. They ensure that AI applications run smoothly and efficiently.

Required Skills:

- Proficiency in scripting and automation.
- Knowledge of containerization and orchestration tools (Docker, Kubernetes).
- Experience with cloud computing platforms (AWS, Azure).
- Monitoring and troubleshooting skills for AI system performance.

The field of AI offers a diverse range of roles, each with its unique responsibilities and skill requirements.

Whether you are interested in machine learning, data science, research, ethics, product management, NLP, computer vision, or DevOps, there is a place for you in the AI industry. Continual learning and staying updated with the latest AI advancements are key to success in this dynamic field.

The Future of Work in the AI Field

The AI field is undergoing a profound transformation, reshaping the nature of work and the skills required for success. Here are some key aspects of the future of work in the AI field:

1. **Increasing Demand for AI Talent:** The demand for AI professionals is surging across industries. Companies are actively seeking individuals with expertise in machine learning, data science, natural language processing, computer vision, and AI ethics. As AI continues to permeate various sectors, the need for skilled practitioners will only grow.

2. **Diverse Range of Roles:** The AI field offers a wide spectrum of roles, from machine learning engineers and data scientists to AI ethicists and product managers. Professionals can choose roles that align with their interests and skills, contributing to the development and deployment of AI solutions.

3. **Interdisciplinary Collaboration:** The future of AI work will involve increased collaboration between AI specialists and experts from other domains. AI engineers will need to work closely with healthcare professionals, economists, biologists, and more to address complex challenges and develop AI applications tailored to specific industries.

4. **Emphasis on Ethical AI:** AI ethics will become a central focus of AI work. Ensuring fairness, transparency, and accountability in AI systems will be essential. AI professionals will need to incorporate ethical considerations into their work and contribute to the responsible development of AI technology.

5. **Continuous Learning and Adaptation:** The AI field evolves rapidly, with new algorithms, frameworks, and technologies emerging regularly. AI professionals will need to engage in continuous learning to stay updated with the latest advancements. This may involve taking online courses, attending workshops, and participating in research communities.

6. **Remote and Flexible Work:** The AI field is conducive to remote work arrangements, allowing professionals to collaborate with teams worldwide. Remote work flexibility will likely remain a prominent feature, enabling individuals to work from diverse locations while contributing to AI projects.

7. **AI for AI:** AI will play a role in enhancing AI development itself. Automated machine learning (AutoML) and AI-assisted coding tools will streamline certain aspects of AI work, making it more accessible to a broader range of professionals.

8. **Impact on Existing Jobs:** AI will augment and transform many existing job roles. While some routine tasks may become automated, AI will create opportunities for individuals to focus on more creative, strategic, and value-added aspects of their work.

The future of work in the AI field promises exciting opportunities and challenges.

AI professionals will need to adapt, embrace interdisciplinary collaboration, prioritize ethics, and engage in lifelong learning to thrive in this dynamic and influential domain.

As technology continues to advance, the AI field will continue to shape the future of work across various industries, offering individuals the chance to contribute to innovative solutions that have a global impact.

www.ingramcontent.com/pod-product-compliance
Lightning Source LLC
Chambersburg PA
CBHW060831290526
45792CB00006BB/1884